George MacDonald's Children's Fantasies and the Divine Imagination

George MacDonald's Children's Fantasies
and the Divine Imagination

Colin Manlove

The Lutterworth Press

For Susan

The Lutterworth Press
P.O. Box 60
Cambridge
CB1 2NT
United Kingdom

www.lutterworth.com
publishing@lutterworth.com

Paperback ISBN: 978 0 7188 9554 9
PDF ISBN: 978 0 7188 4813 2

British Library Cataloguing in Publication Data
A record is available from the British Library

First published by The Lutterworth Press, 2020

Copyright © Colin Manlove, 2019

Published by arrangement
with Cascade Books

All rights reserved. No part of this edition may be reproduced, stored electronically or in any retrieval system, or transmitted in any form or by any means, electronic, mechanical, photocopying, recording, or otherwise, without prior written permission from the Publisher (permissions@lutterworth.com).

Contents

1 Introduction | 1

2 MacDonald's Shorter Fairy Tales: The Various Imagination | 16

3 *At the Back of the North Wind* (**1870**):
The Imagination in the World | 39

4 *The Princess and the Goblin* (**1872**):
The Imagination in the Self | 61

5 *The Wise Woman* (**1875**):
The Imagination against the Self | 79

6 *The Princess and Curdie* (**1882**):
The Imagination against the World | 99

7 Conclusion | 119

Appendix A | 131
Appendix B | 132
Appendix C: Summary of criticism of *The Wise Woman* | 134

Works Cited | 135

1

Introduction

George MacDonald's fairy tales have been children's classics since they first appeared between 1867 and 1882. They include the stories in *Dealings with the Fairies* (1867) and the book-length fantasies *At the Back of the North Wind* (1870), *The Princess and the Goblin* (1872), *The Wise Woman* (1875), and *The Princess and Curdie* (1882). All of them are written for children, and have children as their central characters. In these stories MacDonald created a unique blend of fantasy and realism, and a peculiar depth of mystical vision, inviting us to see our world as continually penetrated by divine forces.

Born in 1824 and raised in Huntly, Aberdeenshire, MacDonald graduated MA in Natural Philosophy (Science) from Aberdeen University in 1845. Though he had hoped to continue his scientific studies abroad, the limitations of family finance drove him to London and a series of tutoring jobs. It was in London that his Christian faith developed as it had not during his repressive Calvinist upbringing. He trained as a Congregationalist in London, and entered on the ministry at Arundel, Sussex in 1851. In the meantime he had met and married Louisa Powell, who was to bear him eleven children and to care for him throughout his lifetime of frequently near-fatal tubercular disease.

MacDonald's life as a minister did not last long. He was expelled in 1853 by the officious officials of his church, who did not like his frequent criticisms of bourgeois greed and materialism, and resented his liberal "German theology" which suggested, for example, that heathens might be saved and animals go to heaven. MacDonald was only one of numbers of the clergy then being expelled from their pulpits by a wave of reactionary orthodoxy in the church. He never resumed a salaried ministry, and devoted much of his life to an unpaid advocacy of his Christian views. This meant that his family had to survive by what MacDonald could earn from writing, preaching, and lecturing, and from family and friends. At first his writings, in poetry (*Within and Without* (1855)) and adult fantasy (*Phantastes* (1858)) did not bring in enough money, but when he took to writing semi-autobiographical realistic novels, such as *Alec Forbes of Howglen* (1865) and *Robert Falconer* (1868), his income and fame increased considerably. Thereafter he was to keep writing novels for the rest of his life. However, his children's fantasy, which became highly popular, also greatly helped to earn him his living.

At the time MacDonald first began writing original fairy tales for children, in the early 1860s, a tradition in Britain for such writing was only some twenty years old. Evangelical and moral cultural attitudes militated against the free use of the imagination in children's books. Not till the 1850s did the fairy tale become more widely accepted as a literary form for children. But still it had to be imbued with explicit moral teaching. The fairy tales of the Grimms had been translated in 1823 and 1826, but were moralized. Mary Howitt's translation of ten Hans Christian Andersen fairy tales, *Wonderful Stories for Children* (1846), is an exception in its refusal to turn tales into lessons. More typical of the period is George Cruikshank's *The Fairy Library* (1853–64), which rewrote a range of traditional fairy stories as temperance and other lessons.

So far as invented fairy tales are concerned, there are several before MacDonald's that stand out. Among those whose influence we see strongly in his work are the Reverend Frances E. Paget's comic-moral *The Hope of the Katzekopfs: or, The Sorrows of Selfishness* (1844), which describes how naughty Prince Eigenwillig (Self-Will) refuses the injunctions of the Fairy Abracadabra and is tormented by the dwarf Selbst (Self) and moralized into submission by old man Discipline. In John Ruskin's *The King of the Golden River* (1851), two brother farmers live in a rich mountain valley until their unkindness insults the natural deities of the locality and brings about their ruin. William Thackeray's "fireside pantomime" *The Rose and the Ring* (1855) is an exuberant parody of fairy tale in which the princely hero Giglio is an ignorant fop and the princess Rosalba a vain coquette whose education the Fairy Blackstick must take in hand before they can

Introduction

qualify for marriage and rule. Frances Browne's *Granny's Wonderful Chair* (1856) is a collection of stories with a mainly rural setting told by a flying chair to keep a king happy. Ordinary folk, from shepherds to fishermen, are the human characters, and goblins, fairies, and elves fill the woods. The ethic is one of natural rather than unnatural behavior. Charles Kingsley's *The Water-Babies* (1863) portrays nature in a marine setting, with Tom the chimney-sweep turned to a small swimming creature who travels downstream to the oceans of the world and beyond, learning how the world is run like a machine by fairies that are sub-vicars of God, and how to become better-behaved.

Of these, *The Hope of the Katzekopfs* is behind the theme of self-love in MacDonald's *The Wise Woman*. The South-West Wind in Ruskin's *King of the Golden River* almost certainly influenced *At the Back of the North Wind*, as did *The Water-Babies*. Thackeray's *The Rose and the Ring* paved the way for "The Light Princess" (1864); and the rural settings and Christian vision of Frances Browne's stories are a strand in all MacDonald's fairy tales.[1]

But MacDonald's sources are wider than these. Several of his fairy tales, such as "The Giant's Heart" and "The Carasoyn," are based on traditional stories. The influence of Perrault seems pervasive, if light; and both Chamisso's *Peter Schlemihl* (1814) and Hans Andersen's stories lie behind "The Shadows." MacDonald, who was fluent in German, is strongly indebted to the earlier invented German Romantic fairy tales of such writers as Goethe, Novalis, Ludwig Tieck, and E. T. A. Hoffmann. Indeed, he valued Friedrich de la Motte Fouqué's *Undine* (1811) as the type of a perfect fairy tale.[2] The idiom and setting of the "Curdie" books recall Tieck; Novalis's influence is noted by MacDonald himself in "The Golden Key"; and something of Hoffmann's metamorphic mockery seems present in "Cross Purposes."

The 1860s, with the popularity of *The Water-Babies* and Lewis Carroll's *Alice in Wonderland* (1865), saw an explosion of English interest in fantasy, particularly for children. MacDonald had been publishing occasional fairy tales since 1862, and he reprinted three of them in his *Adela Cathcart* (1864), a book about the spiritual transformation of a sick girl through storytelling. Seeing the new fashion, in 1867 MacDonald's

---

1. See Manlove, "George MacDonald and the Fairy Tales of Francis Paget and Frances Browne," 17–32.

2. "Were I asked, what is a fairytale? I should reply, *Read Undine: that is a fairytale* ... Of all fairytales I know, I think *Undine* the most beautiful" (MacDonald, "The Fantastic Imagination," *A Dish of Orts*, 313).

publisher Alexander Strahan brought out a collection of five MacDonald tales as *Dealings with the Fairies*, which was reprinted in 1868 and 1890. In 1871, these fairy tales appeared in Strahan's publication of all George MacDonald's fantasy as *Works of Fancy and Imagination*, 10 volumes, which was reprinted continually until 1911.

From the first, MacDonald's fairy tales were felt to be a fine combination of the delights of fairyland with deeper meaning;[3] MacDonald's motto for the *Dealings with the Fairies* was "where more is meant than meets the ear."[4] Most reviewers particularly praised "The Light Princess" for its wit and logic, though MacDonald's friend John Ruskin felt that the swimming episodes in the story were far too suggestively erotic.[5] Lewis Carroll was delighted when he saw "The Light Princess" in manuscript in 1862, and the story is almost certainly behind *Alice in Wonderland*. The notion of a bad fairy's christening curse leaving a princess without a sense of gravity was a wonderful invention, quite following up the complaint of Thackeray's Fairy Blackstick that the usual christening gifts of beauty, charm, wealth, or power did their royal beneficiaries no good whatsoever.[6] "The Shadows," with its continual mixture of grave and gay in its subjects, its overtones of Dickens's "A Christmas Carol" (1843), and its rewriting of Pope's *The Rape of the Lock* with its sylphs, is a sort of literary dance about the central figure Ralph Rinkelmann. In "Cross Purposes," MacDonald produces an unforgettable picture of fairy glamour in a land where streams flow uphill over flowers, trees grow in lakes, owls struggle to read, cats enlarge themselves to cat-a-mountains, and vertiginous towers prove "actually" only two feet high.

Now MacDonald began to write the longer fairy tales *At the Back of the North Wind* and *The Princess and the Goblin*, which were to be instant and enduring successes.[7] MacDonald was also writing more "realistic" and partly autobiographical stories of childhood and boyhood with *Alec Forbes*

---

3. See the contemporary reviews from *The London Review, The British Quarterly Review, The Eclectic Review,* and *The Athenaeum,* reprinted in King and Pierce, eds., *George MacDonald, The Princess and the Goblin and Other Fairy Tales,* 317–19.

4. From Milton, *Il Penseroso,* line 120.

5. Raeper, *George MacDonald,* 222–23.

6. Thackeray, *The Rose and the Ring,* ch. 4.

7. Sample passages from contemporary and later reviews of *The Princess and the Goblin,* taken from *The Saturday Review, Academy, Athenaeum, The Westminster Review,* and *Academy and Literature,* can be found in MacDonald, *The Princess and the Goblin,* King and Pierce, eds., 309–17.

Introduction

of Howglen (1865), the first part of *Robert Falconer* (1868), and *Ranald Bannerman's Boyhood* (1871), all of which sold well for over forty years; as did his novel *Wilfrid Cumbermede* (1872), which is largely a story of boyhood at home and school, and *Sir Gibbie* (1879).

Interestingly MacDonald was no mere exploiter of the fashion for children and for fantasy. Indeed, he believed in the potentially mystical power of both. In his "unspoken" sermon "The Child in the Midst," he said, "God is represented in Jesus, for God is like Jesus: Jesus is represented in the child, for that Jesus is like the child. Therefore God is represented in the child, for that he is like the child. God is child-like."[8] This notion of the child as potentially God-like is seen in many of MacDonald's fairy tales. However, MacDonald discriminates between children who are inherently blessed because they are made in the image of God and those of them who have stained that image with their deeds and thoughts.[9] The purest child is also child-like, that is, innocent in nature. Such "children" MacDonald finds at all ages.

Nevertheless, MacDonald is one of the first writers to put children at the center of his fairy tales. Young Richard and Alice in "Cross Purposes" (1862) predate Charles Kingsley's Tom in *The Water-Babies* and Lewis Carroll's Alice in *Alice in Wonderland*. Prior to MacDonald, most literary fairy tales—Francis Paget's *The Hope of the Katzekopfs*, Ruskin's *The King of the Golden River*, Thackeray's *The Rose and the Ring*, Frances Browne's *Granny's Wonderful Chair*—have young men and women rather than children as their heroes.

Throughout MacDonald's stories we are brought close to the child characters and their feelings. This does not happen so much in *The Water-Babies,* where the adult narrator frequently gets between us and Tom; nor very much in *Alice in Wonderland*, where the creatures are often so freakish as to be on the point of vanishing like the Cheshire Cat, and where Alice's feelings are more at the level of curiosity or irritation than, say, fear or loss. MacDonald creates more or less "realistic" child figures in situations and with reactions we can all understand, even while they are undergoing the strangest of experiences. He makes vivid the terror and exhilaration of Diamond being carried in North Wind's hair as she rushes over the land in a gale. He puts us with Princess Irene as she follows where her grandmother's thread leads her, growing more fearful as her home is left behind and she

---

8. MacDonald, *Unspoken Sermons*, 12.
9. MacDonald, *Unspoken Sermons*, 2–3.

is surrounded by the wild mountain; and still more when the thread leads her right to a small hole in the mountain and then through tunnels in the pitch dark till she loses all sense of direction. The immediacy with which MacDonald puts us close to a child's experience in a fantastic situation is one of his greatest gifts.

As for the mystic power of fantasy, in the epigraph to *Phantastes* (1858) MacDonald quoted the German Romantic writer Novalis (Friedrich von Hardenberg) on the fairy tale: in English this reads: "A fairy tale is like a dream-picture without coherence, a collection of wonderful things and occurrences, e.g. a musical fantasy, the harmonic sequences of the Aeolian harp, nature itself."[10] This remained MacDonald's view of the fairy tale in his late essay "The Fantastic Imagination," his introduction to *The Light Princess and Other Fairy Tales* (New York: G. P. Putnams, 1893), where he speaks of it as inherently mysterious in essence and musical in its working; for "The greatest forces lie in the region of the uncomprehended."[11] And here MacDonald brings together his idea of the fairy tale with his idea of the childlike: "For my part, I do not write for children, but for the childlike, whether of five, or fifty, or seventy-five."[12] Such readers remain innocent in that they do not try to explain the fairy tale away, but remain "still and let it work on that part of them for whose sake it exists."[13] MacDonald is the first British writer to give fantasy such a high place in literature.

For MacDonald, as for Novalis, fantasy is largely the product of the unconscious imagination. MacDonald believed that God lived in the roots of the imagination, "in the chamber of our being in which the candle of our consciousness goes out in darkness, and sends forth from thence wonderful gifts into the light of that understanding which is His candle."[14] The fairy tale especially, being created by and in this imagination, is therefore grounded in divine mystery. Through it God speaks to us, even if we do not always recognize his voice.

This belief that God actually lives in the imagination of man and is the author of man's creativity is perhaps the most striking feature of MacDonald's thought. It is first advanced by him in an essay "The Imagination: Its Functions and Its Culture" in 1867, the same year in which his mystical

---

10. Novalis, *Die Fragmente*, in *Schriften*, III, 572 # 113.
11. MacDonald, "The Fantastic Imagination," *A Dish of Orts*, 319.
12. MacDonald, "The Fantastic Imagination," *A Dish of Orts*, 317.
13. MacDonald, "The Fantastic Imagination," *A Dish of Orts*, 321–22.
14. MacDonald, "The Imagination," *A Dish of Orts*, 25.

Introduction

fairy tale "The Golden Key" first appeared. Though this view has its antecedents in ideas of divine *afflatus* in the prophets, in Greek poetics, Ficino, Sir Philip Sidney, Milton, and perhaps most notably Blake, none of these saw God as actually taking up residence within the mind of man. It makes reading MacDonald's fairy tales a potentially mystical experience; and it gives them a potentially bottomless significance. At any point the world in them will drop away and reveal endless gulfs beneath or around. The very image of this is found in the Curdie books, where a seeming bath becomes an ocean of stars, or the walls of a room disappear to reveal the night sky, or a spinning wheel is transformed to a giant wheel of fire.

Why did MacDonald have this view of God as being at the root of the human imagination? One answer may be that because the imagination is the most mysterious faculty in man, and at home with infinity and infinite depths of thought and suggestion, it is nearest in character to God. Another could be precisely that the imagination's roots lie beyond knowledge, and we cannot tell if the mystic depths it seems to reach are truth or subjective illusion. This was the problem for the Romantic poets, exemplified in Wordsworth's "egotistical sublime." What MacDonald may be doing is removing the potential subjectivity of the imagination by placing God, or ultimate reality, at its very center. In this way, the visions sent up to him from it would be *given*, not self-made.

MacDonald also believed that the world itself was made by God's creative imagination. Therefore, the world, properly seen—and that means seen imaginatively and mystically—is also a fairy tale. This implies that in order to write about reality most truly, one should write fairy tales as Novalis describes them. However, man is independent and able to choose for himself the form in which to embody his ideas. God thinks man's thoughts, and thinks the world into being: but man has still himself to find from nature the perfect expression of his thought.[15] What the human being does is discover in nature the God-given material that best realizes or expresses his thought. This is why MacDonald asks, "Is not the *Poet*, the *Maker*, a less suitable name for him than the *Trouvère*, the *Finder*?"[16]

In most of his fairy tales for children, MacDonald did not write quite as chaotically as the quotation from Novalis might suggest: he did not too often "assail the soul of his reader as the wind assails an aeolian harp."[17] He

---

15. MacDonald, "The Imagination," *A Dish of Orts*, 18.
16. MacDonald, "The Imagination," *A Dish of Orts*, 20.
17. MacDonald, "The Fantastic Imagination," *A Dish of Orts*, 321.

left such unmixed mystery to his adult romances *Phantastes* (1858) and *Lilith* (1895) and to one visionary fairy tale, "The Golden Key" (1867). Rather, the mysteries he gives us are more occasional, breaking through the story to reveal another and deeper narrative running parallel to it. In *At the Back of the North Wind*, for example, young Diamond's life as a London cab-man's son is interrupted from time to time by a great lady who calls herself the North Wind. She takes Diamond on a journey round the city and then to the North Pole, so that he may reach the country at her back. In this way, Diamond sees the forces that govern the world, such as pain, poverty, and death, and the yet deeper reality that somehow resolves them all in an approaching universal song.

Indeed, several of the shorter fairy tales are not evidently mystical at all. Such are "Cross Purposes," "The Giant's Heart," "The Carasoyn," "The Light Princess," and "Little Daylight," which are re-creations or parodies of traditional folk stories. The last two have some Christian overtones, as we shall see: but with the exception of "The Shadows" and "The Golden Key," the shorter fairy tales seem to be more secular in emphasis. However, we should be careful here, for Friedrich de la Motte Fouqué's *Undine* (1814), regarded by MacDonald as the perfect fairy tale, seems on first glance concerned only with the this-worldly issues of a man's gain and then loss of a female water-spirit. Yet further thought may lead us to see in it the theme of the loss of a man's soul; or, in the words of Charlotte Yonge,

> Though in this tale there is far less of spiritual meaning than in [Fouqué's] *Sintram*, we cannot but see that Fouqué's thought was that the grosser human nature [of the knight Huldbrand who leaves Undine for a human bride] is unable to appreciate what is absolutely pure and unearthly.[18]

"The imagination," MacDonald tells us, "is that faculty which gives form to thought."[19] The thought, or idea comes first, and then the image that best expresses it. That image will be more or less apt in conveying the thought according to the skill of the creator. God, who thought and then created the universe out of nothing, had no existent image in which to embody that thought: but he who is the fount of all contained all thoughts and images together. Man, however, has to seek the image in nature. Thus, so far as man is concerned, MacDonald's view is Platonist: *first* the thought, *then*

18. Yonge, Introduction to Fouqué, *Sintram and His Companions*, 2. See also Manlove, "George MacDonald and Friedrich de la Motte Fouqué."

19. MacDonald, "The Imagination," *A Dish of Orts*, 2.

Introduction

the material that will best express it. This is close to Sir Philip Sidney's idea that the poet "doth not learn a conceit out of a matter but maketh matter for a conceit":[20] and indeed MacDonald's ideas on creation are often near to those of Renaissance Neoplatonism.

For some would argue that the image comes first, not the idea or "fore-conceit." Coleridge did not start with an idea in creating "Kubla Khan" (1797) or *The Ancient Mariner* (1798), but with a pleasure dome, a deep cavern, a ship going far southwards to the ice. Later his intellect insisted that "Kubla Khan" was unfinished and added elucidatory marginal comments to *The Ancient Mariner*. Similarly, William Cowper in *Yardley Oak* (1791) struggles to draw moral lessons from a huge and ancient oak tree that fascinates him. Or C. S. Lewis tells us that all his stories began with a picture—a lion, a ship coming out of a picture, a floating island, or simply a girl looking in a shop window—and then he had to think out a story in which they could exist. And MacDonald himself may well have started *The Princess and the Goblin* from the picture of an old lady living forgotten in an attic; and have begun *At the Back of the North Wind* from the image of a little boy sleeping in a draughty hayloft.

Others would say that dividing thought from image is in any case a mistake. The image comes carrying its idea with it. Some images convey joy, some beauty, others despair or horror. True, at some point far back in time men made these various images express these ideas. But the point is that for the artist the world is already full of conferred thought. Thus Shelley uses the idea of the ever-moving wind to picture his own yearning spirit; or T. S. Eliot uses the idea of a wasted land to portray a world that has lost meaning.

But the question comes to what MacDonald meant by "thought" and what by "form." The thought is a movement of the mind that can only reach expression through a form. Mathematics requires numbers and symbols, chemistry needs formulae, history needs evidence, philosophy speaks in arguments, art in images, music in sounds, literature in words. For MacDonald, all original thoughts belong to the imagination. "The construction of any hypothesis whatever is the work of the imagination."[21] However, putting thought into form and thus creating art and furthering knowledge is not, for MacDonald, the sole concern of the imagination. For him it has a higher purpose, "which springs from man's immediate relation to the

---

20. Sidney, "A Defence of Poesy" (1583), 435.
21. MacDonald, "The Imagination," *A Dish of Orts*, 13.

Father, that of following and finding out the divine imagination in whose image it was made."[22] This involves tracing God through his creation, that is, through the whole range of nature. Indeed, this higher purpose must be combined with that of putting thought into form. And here the imagination alone will lead us to truth. The use of intellectual proofs of God's existence—such as those of William Paley, who argued from a nature that appeared to run like a watch to a great Watchmaker, from observed design to a universal Designer—are rejected by MacDonald.

So much for what the imagination *does*: but what exactly *is* it? For MacDonald, it is clearly a part of the mind different from the intellect. Although the imagination cannot work without the intellect, the latter is inferior: "the Intellect must labour, workman-like, under the direction of the architect, Imagination."[23] MacDonald sees the imagination as man's highest mental faculty, for if used aright, it alone can bring us close to God. Indeed, God himself lives in the depths of each man's imagination, "and sends forth from thence wonderful gifts into the light of that understanding which is his candle."[24] To follow and find out the divine imagination can therefore involve a journey into the regions of one's unconscious mind. When little Princess Irene meets her great-great grandmother in the attics of her house, she has made a journey not just up several stairs in a house, but up several stairs in her mind. At first Irene sees the old lady as a withered crone, but on subsequent meetings she appears younger and more beautiful, showing that Irene has got closer to her true divine nature.

But equally, the further one goes *out* of oneself to enter into sympathy with nature, the closer also one comes to a divine reality. To see the truth of a flower, one must see with the imagination, which rejoices in the thing for itself, not for the scientific facts about it: "The idea of God *is* the flower; his idea is not the botany of the flower."[25] God's imagination turned thought into form when it made the flower, which speaks his joy and awakens longing. In coming close in love to the flower we come close to the God who made it.

> The truth *of a thing*, then, is the blossom of it, the thing it is made for, the topmost stone set on with rejoicing; truth in a man's imagination is the power to recognise this truth of a thing; and

---

22. MacDonald, "The Imagination," *A Dish of Orts*, 10.
23. MacDonald, "The Imagination," *A Dish of Orts*, 11.
24. MacDonald, "The Imagination," *A Dish of Orts*, 25.
25. MacDonald, *Unspoken Sermons*, 466.

wherever, in anything that God has made, in the glory of it, be it sky or flower or human face, we see the glory of God, there a true imagination is beholding a truth of God.[26]

In part, this going out of oneself into the things that God has made is described in *At the Back of the North Wind*, where young Diamond makes a friend of the lady North Wind and is shown the nature of the world. Here the truth is both joy and pain for Diamond, who is shown some of the suffering and apparent injustice in the world, both natural and human, and comes to understand something of the love that both fills and transcends it.

The imagination is not all good, however, only the loving and innocent imagination that is infused with God. When the young man Anodos in *Phantastes* enters Fairy Land, which is his own imagination, he is sufficiently open to evil to meet there a devouring Ash Tree or a wonder-slaying shadow that attaches itself to him. When Vane in *Lilith* enters a desert world populated in part by monsters, he has entered this world as his evil spirit sees it. Such horrors can fill the imagination when we are ignorant of the God at its root. MacDonald says, "If the dark portion of our own being were the origin of our imaginations, we might well fear the apparition of such monsters as would be generated in the sickness of a decay which could never feel—only declare—a slow return towards primeval chaos. But the Maker is our Light."[27] The monsters of the Bad Burrow are about to devour Vane when the moonlight that is God at the center of his imagination reappears and renders them impotent once more. The evil people of Gwyntystorm in *The Princess and Curdie* see the grotesque beasts that accompany Curdie as terrors, but Curdie, who lives within divine truth, knows that their shapes hide souls on the way from evil to good.

All MacDonald's fairy tales involve journeys into the imagination. Irene going upstairs to the attics, Curdie coming to believe in the reality of Irene's "grandmother," Diamond travelling with North Wind, wicked Princess Rosamond being taken away by the wise woman from her palace to a cottage in a wilderness—these are all going out of their everyday selves into the deepest regions of their natures. And the same can be said of the shorter tales—Mossy in "The Golden Key" going to find the golden key at one end of a rainbow, and then travelling with Tangle to the other end; the princess in "Little Daylight" entering the dark forest where she will find her love; Richard and Alice in "Cross Purposes" becoming lost in Fairyland; the

26. MacDonald, *Unspoken Sermons*, 469.
27. MacDonald, "The Imagination," *A Dish of Orts*, 25.

prince in "The Light Princess" slowly sinking beneath the water of the lake to remove the evil enchantment; even Buffy-Bob and Tricksy-Wee finding their way into the magic realm of the giants. In the late fairy tale "The History of Photogen and Nycteris" (1879), we have a reversal: the girl Nycteris, enclosed from childhood by a witch in a dark room lit only dimly by a lamp, one day accidentally escapes into the real night, lit by a moon that far transcends the lamp she once took it for. She has emerged from a fantastic world she thought was real into a real one that she takes to be fantastic. In so doing she is opened both to her imagination and to the wonder of the world that most of us take for granted.

The imagination is indeed the subject of all MacDonald's children's fantasies. In all of them it is the only way to see the world aright, because the world of the spirit is at its heart. If we enter it without love, however, we will meet the images of our own truancies. In all his fantasies also, MacDonald explores different aspects of the imagination, showing it under different conditions and at shifting levels. In *The Princess and the Goblin*, he shows it as part of the mind, alongside other and humbler faculties. The nature of the divine imagination that made the world is the subject of *At the Back of the North Wind*, together with a child's imaginative life within the world. *The Wise Woman* shows the attempt to make bad children reform enough to enter their imaginations. And in *The Princess and Curdie* the imagination takes arms against the evil of a materialist city: here, with a whole society gone bad, there is seems no room for reform, and destruction is made the only remedy.

In MacDonald's view the fairy tale is endless in significance, because like the imagination it originates in God. In "The Fantastic Imagination," he declares, "A genuine work of art must mean many things; the truer its art, the more things it will mean."[28] Because "it is God's things, his embodied thoughts, which alone a man has to use, modified and adapted to his own purposes, for the expression of his thoughts," "[a] man may well discover truth in what he wrote; for he was dealing all the time with things that came from thoughts beyond his own."[29] Therefore, if we think, say, that "The Giant's Heart" is only a child's tale of escape from a giant, or that "Cross Purposes" is simply a picture of the illusions of fairy land, we may be ignoring a wealth of deeper experience in these stories.

---

28. MacDonald, "The Fantastic Imagination," *A Dish of Orts*, 317.

29. MacDonald, "The Fantastic Imagination," *A Dish of Orts*, 320, 321.

Introduction

One says "experience," because MacDonald's notion of the meaning of a story is not always a formulated one. He allows that "the fairytale would give no delight" did it not have truth in it, and that each reader will legitimately read his or her meaning into it. He also says that one meaning may be better than another; and that a reader's interpretation may even be better than that of the artist himself.[30] But he also says that the fairy tale is not an allegory with a set meaning: it works indirectly like a sonata, where there may be agreement as to its broad direction, but none where it comes to specific interpretation. While acknowledging the rightful place of intellectual interpretation, MacDonald says that "The greatest forces lie in the region of the uncomprehended"[31]; and

> If a writer's aim be logical conviction, he must spare no pains, not merely to be understood, but to escape being misunderstood; where his object is to move by suggestion, to cause to imagine, then let him assail the soul of his reader as the wind assails an aeolian harp. If there be music in my reader, I would gladly wake it. Let fairytale of mine go for a firefly that now flashes, now is dark, but may flash again.[32]

This separation of the intellectual from the emotional in literature seems a little sharp, for it is quite possible to have both kinds of experience at once. But in moving from the sonata to the aeolian harp as his analogy for the fairy tale, MacDonald has moved away from something still structured enough to allow us to find patterns in it to a mode that refuses the intelligence any place in response. "The best way with music, I imagine, is not to bring the forces of our intellect to bear upon it, but to be still and let it work on that part of us for whose sake it exists."[33] This is because the fairy tale ultimately deals with what is beyond words. Nevertheless, it is composed in words: and that, ultimately, must work against any musical analogy.[34]

However, the Romantic side of MacDonald, the side that often led him to attack the very scientific method in which he was educated, less happily pushes him on here to say that the intellect is the enemy of true understanding: "We spoil countless precious things by intellectual greed."

30. MacDonald, "The Fantastic Imagination," *A Dish of Orts*, 316–17.
31. MacDonald, "The Fantastic Imagination," *A Dish of Orts*, 319.
32. MacDonald, "The Fantastic Imagination," *A Dish of Orts*, 321.
33. MacDonald, "The Fantastic Imagination," *A Dish of Orts*, 321–22.
34. Manlove, "George MacDonald's Fairy Tales," 102–4.

This is followed by a somewhat sentimental attack on those who chose to be intellectual adults rather than children: such, MacDonald declares, will become vain "little men," that is, dwarfs.[35]

MacDonald ends his essay on "The Fantastic Imagination" by seeing his best readers as passive ones, who let the fairy tale play on their naked spirits without interposing anything of their impertinent minds or selves. Such readers will let the fairy tale work most deeply on their souls, and be moved without knowing why: "If any strain of my 'broken music' make a child's eyes flash, or his mother's grow for a moment dim, my labour will not have been in vain." This is a noble aim, and it is probably the deepest working of MacDonald's fairy tales: but it reduces the reader to privacy, unable to articulate and share literary experience with others, except through tear-filled intimacy. And earlier in the essay MacDonald has given the intelligence of his readers a role in tracing the many meanings of fairy tale. It is clear that he himself as an intelligent man is torn on this subject. All one can say is that there is ultimately no reconciliation between the reader who puts the mystery of the fairy tale first and the reader who tries to understand it. For the one is looking into the deeps, and the other is trying to bring something up from the depths to the light; the second is valuing man's understanding, where the first is leaving man behind.

This of course has implications for the very writing of this book. Here you will find what are largely intellectual interpretations, attempts to find patterns in often mystifying material. It is hoped that this process does not involve "intellectual greed," and does not spoil any of these stories, but rather enhances them. The mind need not be at odds with emotion in reading fairy tales if it finds new wonders there. For "the region of the uncomprehended" there are no words, only the mute mystic experience MacDonald settles on at the close of his essay: but we can at least show how it is presented.

The subject of this book is the imagination in MacDonald's fairy tales, just as it was MacDonald's subject when discussing both fairy tales and the mind. Starting with the shorter tales we will see how they show a range of types of the imagination, before we explore particular treatments of that faculty in the longer stories. Broadly, the four longer children's fairy tales divide into two kinds. *At the Back of the North Wind* and *The Princess and the Goblin* show what position the imagination has, first within the *world*, and then within the *self*. The next two books, *The Wise Woman* and *The*

---

35. MacDonald, "The Fantastic Imagination," *A Dish of Orts*, 322.

Princess and Curdie, describe the imagination trying to *change* the world and the self. The first two are about *being*, the next two about *doing*. In this way, MacDonald's children's fantasy covers the whole range of the imagination's nature and operations.

What we are dealing with here is one of the great masters of children's fantasy, an inventor of much of its character and a writer of a profound vision in which the childlike is at the very center of the fairy tale as a picture of the universe. As MacDonald's son Greville writes in his biography, "My father's knowledge as to what food children best thrive upon came from his own child-like faith in their celestial inheritance."[36]

---

36. Greville MacDonald, *George MacDonald and His Wife*, 362.

2

MacDonald's Shorter Fairy Tales
The Various Imagination

MacDonald's shorter children's fairy tales were all written at different times across nearly twenty years, and for different occasions. "Cross Purposes" first appeared in *Beeton's Christmas Annual* for 1862, "The Giant's Heart" in the Christmas number of the *Illustrated London News* for 1863; and both these and "The Shadows" and "The Light Princess" were published in *Adela Cathcart* (1864), where they featured as stories told to help restore the mentally sick Adela to her true self. *The Golden Key* made its debut with the other four of MacDonald's fairy stories in his collection *Dealings with the Fairies* (1867). The long story "The Carasoyn" was published in two parts, the first as "The Fairy Fleet—An English Märchen" in *The Argosy in* April 1866, and the second as "The Fairy Cobbler" in *Good Cheer* (December 25, 1867) before appearing as one story in MacDonald's collected *Works of Fancy and Imagination* (10 vols.; 1871). "Little Daylight" came as an inset story in *At the Back of the North Wind* (1870) told by Mr Raymond to the patients in the children's hospital. "Photogen and Nycteris: A Day and Night Mährchen" (often reprinted as "The Day Boy and the Night Girl") appeared in the Christmas number of *The Graphic*, 1879. All of these stories were collected in *The Light Princess and Other Fairy Tales*, published by G. P. Putnam's of New York in 1893, which thereafter became the standard text. The tales were thus written at different times in MacDonald's experience, for different readerships, and in very different publications. For example, "The Light Princess" was shared with Lewis Carroll during its writing, when MacDonald's children were young and the family still growing; and "Photogen and Nycteris" appeared when MacDonald was mourning the deaths within a year of his beloved daughter Mary in 1878 and his son Maurice in 1879.

These "shorter" fairy tales are still much longer than anything in Grimm or Andersen (apart from "The Snow Queen"). If we take *The Complete Fairy Tales*, edited by U. C. Knoepflmacher (Penguin, 1999), "Little Daylight" has fifteen pages, "Cross Purposes" sixteen, "The Giant's Heart" eighteen, "The Golden Key" twenty-four, "The Shadows" twenty-six, "The Carasoyn" thirty-five, "Photogen and Nycteris" thirty-seven, and "The Light Princess" thirty-eight. (In the same volume *The Wise Woman* has sixty-eight pages.) "The Carasoyn" was originally twenty pages until MacDonald added a second part a year later.[1] The greater length of MacDonald's stories comes from their inclusion of characterization, descriptions of scenery, feelings, reflections, and not infrequently digressions; whereas in, say, the Grimms' stories the essence is the plot, which reduces everything else. But MacDonald's stories also differ greatly in length from one another: and here the reason is that the longer tales such as "The Shadows," "The Light Princess," "The Golden Key," and "Photogen and Nycteris," deal with a process of gradual spiritual change in their central figures.

That MacDonald is not writing to any formula is seen in the changing natures of the tales. The first, "Cross Purposes," has aspects of traditional fairy story motifs, with a fairy queen who wants to abduct mortals (as in "Thomas the Rhymer" and "Tam Lin") and fairy illusion or glamour being used to effect this. The giant story with the separate heart is clearly traditional in origin. And stories about princesses and suitors are common in oral literature; though apart from their social setting, MacDonald's "Princess" stories are utterly different in character and interest from any traditional story. Much nearer again to folktale is "The Carasoyn," set in the Scottish countryside and then south Devon, with a fairy fleet, preposterous magical requests, and a granted wish that causes the fairy queen nothing but misery. In amongst these varyingly traditional stories are published the Andersen-like "The Shadows," the mystical journey of "The Golden Key," and in "Photogen and Nycteris" the story of two children kept isolated in the dark and the light respectively. MacDonald retains the fairy-tale frame for these three stories, but it is relatively perfunctory. In "The Shadows," Ralph Rinkelmann is made king of the fairies, but we soon drop these for

---

1. Shaberman, *George MacDonald*, 45.

the tribe of shadows. We are told that the fairies drive Tangle out of her house in "The Golden Key," but we hear nothing more of them. The wicked fairy Watho sets up the extreme predicaments of the girl and boy in "Photogen and Nycteris," but the two children develop on their own during the story.

Compared to these, three of the longer fairy tales for children—the two books about the Princess Irene and Curdie, and *The Wise Woman* (all first written between 1871 and 1877)—seem relatively consistent in the semi-medieval/magical worlds in which they are set. In terms of their royal worlds, only "The Light Princess" and "Little Daylight" could also be seen as belonging to this group.

MacDonald's shorter fairy tales are distinguished from those of book-length by their tendency to have a single clear objective, whether it is to escape from a giant or a witch, rescue a princess from a curse, find the lock for a golden key, or get hold of a bottle of Carasoyn. In the book-length stories there is no such clear aim; in form they are more desultory, in plot occasional. The wind in *At the Back of the North Wind*, for instance, has no purpose with Diamond save to show him what she does in the world; and he is without her for much of the second half of the book. The plots of the goblins in *The Princess and the Goblin* are only gradually revealed, and the growing relationship of Princess Irene with her increasingly strange "grandmother" is at least as important.

Although these eight fairy tales have, either individually or in clusters, formed the subjects of numerous critical accounts, so far little has been produced on them as a whole group.[2] And while many essays have appeared on the complex "The Golden Key" or "The Light Princess," little has been written on, say, "Little Daylight," "The Shadows," or "The Carasoyn." For all the diversity in character of these stories, MacDonald seems to have thought of them all as belonging together: the Putnam's edition of 1893 has his imprimatur, in the shape of an introduction in which he describes his view of the fairy tale. It also is perhaps significant that the publication in 1867 of the first five stories as *Dealings with the Fairies* coincided with the appearance in the same year of his essay, "The Imagination: Its Functions and Its Culture,"[3] which casts light on the origin and nature of these tales. As we shall see the tales all have some form of the imagination as their

---

2. There are accounts of them in terms of sub-groups: see Appendix A.

3. In the July issue of the *British Quarterly Review* (Shaberman, *George MacDonald*, 71).

central concern. It may be added that MacDonald's essays on the imagination and the fairy tale form almost the only commentary we have on his own work and outlook: he had little to say on the novel form in which he wrote so much.

This concern with the imagination is not at first so readily discernible as it is, say, in MacDonald's adult fantasy *Phantastes*. There Anodos says he woke up to find his bedroom changing into a glade in Fairy Land. It is easy then to say that he has not woken into "real life" but into a dream, and that he is still asleep in bed. (He is actually described as twice waking, at the beginnings of chapters 1 and 2.) But while there are occasional transitions from sleep to waking in the shorter fairy tales, more commonly we see characters who are wide awake entering other worlds, as when Mossy and Tangle go into fairyland in "The Golden Key" or Buffy-Bob and Tricksy-Wee in "The Selfish Giant" find their way through the forest near their home to the house of the giant and his wife. Further, in the shorter tales there is not just one central character as with Anodos, which suggests subjectivity, but usually two, a boy and a girl, or a princess and a prince. (The only exception here is "The Shadows," where old Ralph Rinkelmann is alone in his meetings with the shadows, and this story has much of the shifting, directionless, dreaming quality of *Phantastes*.)

How then do the tales show that we have moved into the imagination? One of the means is by breaking up a settled state or assumption, implying a move away from the rational level. This is a device found in much literature, from *Oedipus Rex* to *King Lear*, and from *Gulliver's Travels* to *Alice in Wonderland*, where a sudden disjunction of behavior, context, or action opens up a wilder or madder world beneath the "normal" one. In MacDonald's fantasy it is often done by the disruption of a house. In *Phantastes* the hero's bedroom turns to a glade in Fairy Land, and in *Lilith* Mr Vane finds that the attic of his house has become a route to the region of the seven dimensions. In each case, the house (as in Edgar Allan Poe's stories) is a symbol of the structured and known mind, suddenly exposed to the unknown depths within itself: Vane says, "'If I know nothing of my own garret . . . what is there to secure me against my own brain?'"[4] So in the fairy tales we have evil fairies who appear in palaces to curse christenings ("The Light Princess," "Little Daylight"), shadows who crowd into the room of a sick man ("The Shadows"), children who blunder into an ogre's house ("The Giant's Heart"), a stream made to run through a cottage ("The

---

4. MacDonald, *Phantastes and Lilith*, 198.

Carasoyn"), and children abducted from their homes by fairies ("Cross Purposes," "The Golden Key").

Also suggesting the imagination, Fairyland borders the realms of men, like the unconscious beside the conscious mind; and young people are readily drawn into it. The very idea of having two worlds—the ordinary one and the fairy one, which someone enters—is relatively new in modern English literary fantasy:[5] it is first introduced by William Morris in "Lindenborg Pool" (1856) and by MacDonald himself in *Phantastes* (1858). In "The Golden Key," both children's houses are beside the wood that borders Fairyland, and indeed the garden of Mossy (who is to prove the more native to Fairyland) has some "straggling trees" sent into it.[6] In "The Light Princess," the prince is lost (often a sign of going into the unconscious mind in MacDonald's fiction) in a forest before he comes upon the princess; and in "Little Daylight," which is in some ways another version of the same story, the palace is also surrounded by a wild wood, this time full of fairies, and again the prince is lost. The giant in "The Giant's Heart" "lived on the borders of Giantland where it touched on the country of common people" (81). In "Cross Purposes" we learn that "No mortal, or fairy either, can tell where Fairyland begins and where it ends. But somewhere on the borders of Fairyland there was a nice country village, in which lived some nice country people" (104): not surprisingly, with all this respectability, a group of fairies set about stealing two "nice" children from thence, one of whom proves not so nice for them. "The Carasoyn" has a fairy fleet sailing through young Colin's cottage-home, down the channel he has cut to release the stream: the fleet anchors at night and there begins a fairy revel which Colin can watch from his bed. This is an image of his "dreaming" and seeing with his unconscious imagination, something he is particularly able to do: "Colin had no need of fairy ointment to anoint his eyes and make him able to see fairies. Most people need this; but Colin was naturally gifted" (221).

The fairy tales also take us away from the world of reason and order by often beginning with the inversion of a natural law. Of course, all fairy tales, in using magic, alter or suspend natural laws—as in seven-league

---

5. But it is native to all Scottish fantasy. Indeed many of the characteristics of MacDonald's fantasy discussed here are so too. For generally MacDonald's and Scottish fantasy belong to the European subversive mode rather than to the more usually conservative English tradition. See my *Scottish Fantasy Literature* (1994) and *The Fantasy Literature of England* (1999).

6. MacDonald, *The Complete Fairy Tales*, ed., Knoepflmacher, 121. References throughout this chapter are to this edition.

boots, cloaks of invisibility, flying horses, geese that lay gold pieces, giants or midgets (Tom Thumb). But MacDonald's fairy tales draw our attention to the normality that is being flouted. His one tale that comes specifically from a folk tale, "The Giant's Heart," involves a giant having put his heart out to be nursed by a savage eagle: the element of the grotesque heightens the suspension of natural law.[7] In other tales, we have a princess whose gravity is removed (in both senses); another who wakes at night and sleeps by day ("Little Daylight"); shadows without substance ("The Shadows") or visible source ("The Golden Key"); one child who knows nothing of day and another ignorant of night ("Photogen and Nycteris"); a fairy stream that defies nature as it flows across the country ("Cross Purposes"). These inversions help transport us from a stable and predictable world into a much more uncertain and fluid one.

Part of this comes from the way the tales are often whimsically motivated. In "The Shadows," the fairies take it into their heads that they need a king and choose the near-dead Ralph Rinkelmann, who then meets some of his lesser-known subjects, the Shadows, who show him their lives and take him to their church in Iceland. The story passes from event to event with little causal connection among them. In "The Golden Key" the story can seem a series of episodes strung together.[8] Mossy at first wants his dinner, then the key at the end of the rainbow; then he is bid look for the keyhole, but also discovers another desire, to find "the country whence the shadows fall." Meanwhile we follow another narrative of the girl Tangle, who has at first few motives at all, and who need not have chosen to accompany Mossy on his journey. Her history is "entangled" with his for only part of the story, for she follows a quite different and more indirect route at its end, and for no immediately clear reason.

Similar arbitrariness is found in other tales. What is the point of making a princess lose her gravity? Why is Little Daylight cursed with having to sleep all day, wake all night, and wax and wane with the moon? What, in "Photogen and Nycteris," is the witch Watho's interest in making one child

---

7. In the version of the story in Dasent, *Popular Tales from the Norse*, 47–58, to which MacDonald was probably indebted, the concealment of the heart is simply a *donnée*, and the concern is much more with finding where the giant has hidden it than with making a known hiding-place questionable.

8. Cynthia Marshall, "Reading 'The Golden Key,'" 99, finds the story "repeatedly . . . on the verge of concluding," as does Robert Lee Wolff, *The Golden Key*, 135–38. Richard Reis, *George MacDonald's Fiction*, 79, feels that many of the incidents could be omitted without subverting the plot.

know only day, and the other only night? Why in "The Giant's Heart" has Giant Thunderthump put his heart out for protection, when his wife tells him she could perfectly well look after it at home? What makes the fairy queen in "The Carasoyn" ask for "'something that I neither like nor please —that I don't know anything about'" (195), particularly as, when she gets it, it makes her and all the fairies old and unhappy? Further, what is the point of all the strange tasks Colin has to perform in order to get it for her? And in "Cross Purposes" the choice of particular mortals to visit the fairy court seems virtually motiveless, and leads nowhere.

All these dislocating devices serve to warn us that we are in the realm of the imagination, where sense and sequence do not exist in rational terms, where known laws are turned upside down and the self becomes part of a landscape outside time and space. But as said, there is a difference here with *Phantastes*, where the world is seen subjectively, through the imagination of the solitary hero. The children, princes, and princesses of the short fairy tales are named, there is more than one hero and the world is as much outside as inside the characters. We seem to be dealing with a much more objective world.

However this difference, while felt, is not a final one. As seen, for MacDonald, the world and the human mind are interchangeable, because everything, "mind" and "body" alike, is made out of God's imagination. "The imagination of man is made in the image of the imagination of God . . . in which the imagination of man lives and moves and has its being."[9] "The world is the human being turned inside out. All that moves in the mind is symbolized in nature."[10] Each, the "outside" world and the world made by the human imagination, is ultimately symbolic of the other, because both are created by the imagination of God. Therefore, a fairy story, an imaginary story, may in its narrative of "physical" adventures in the outer world also be symbolically describing adventures in the mind. This, it will be argued here is precisely what is happening in MacDonald's shorter fairy tales.[11] However diverse they are in character, written at scattered points in

9. MacDonald, "The Imagination," *A Dish of Orts*, 3.

10. MacDonald, "The Imagination," *A Dish of Orts*, 9. Compare Novalis, *Schriften*, II, 377 # 617, from whom MacDonald may have taken this idea: "Was ausser mir ist, ist gerade in mir, ist mein—und umgek[ehrt]" ("What is outside me is in fact inside me—is mine—and vice versa").

11. The point has occasionally been made before, as by Mendelson, "The Fairy Tales of George MacDonald," 39 in relation to "The Golden Key," but has never been followed through.

his literary life, long or short, comic or serious, they all take place within the imagination, and are dramas enacted among its various aspects.

It is just these "various aspects" that are going to be our concern here. For MacDonald views the human imagination as no single or always pure thing. In his adult romances *Phantastes* and *Lilith* it contains monsters as readily as angels. MacDonald sees the imagination as operating in several modes, some good, some not so good. These are fancy; delusion; perversion; creation; spiritual insight; and vision. Taken together, MacDonald's shorter fairy tales explore these various aspects of the imagination.

What are the characteristics of these different modes? MacDonald sees fancy as the imagination at play, finding "strange resemblances between external things" rather than presenting "the direct embodiment of idea in form."[12] Delusion is the mutating shape of Fairy in "The Carasoyn," while Colin struggles to keep hold of her. Perversion is the evil imagination, "the dark portion of our own being," which generates "monsters" and "a slow return towards primeval chaos."[13] In contrast, creation is the imagination working in the image of the imagination of God, putting thought into form to embody truth.[14] The imagination of spiritual insight, "seeking the ideal in everything, will elevate them to their true and noble service": such "outgoing of the imagination is one with aspiration, and will do more to elevate above what is low and vile than all possible inculcations of morality."[15] As for the visionary imagination, it is that which approaches as near as it can to God, who is immediately active at the root of the imagination itself.

One of MacDonald's most frequent points concerning the "good" or creative imagination is that it works by law:

> The mind of man is the product of live Law; it thinks by law, it dwells in the midst of law, it gathers from law its growth; with law, therefore, can it work to any result. . . . Obeying law, the maker works like his creator; not obeying law, he is such a fool as heaps a pile of stones and calls it a church.[16]

This may seem strange in view of the anti-rational, dislocated aspects we just have seen of MacDonald's fairy tales: and indeed the extent to which

---

12. MacDonald, "Shelley" (1860), *A Dish of Orts*, 279–80.
13. MacDonald, "The Imagination," *A Dish of Orts*, 25.
14. MacDonald, "The Imagination," *A Dish of Orts*, 2–4.
15. MacDonald, "The Imagination," *A Dish of Orts*, 30.
16. MacDonald, "The Fantastic Imagination," *A Dish of Orts*, 315.

he returns to the point, in both his 1867 essay on "The Imagination" and his 1893 essay "The Fantastic Imagination," suggests a certain tension between his advocacy of incoherence and mystery and his wish for discipline and control. For MacDonald, the key would lie in the different kinds of the imagination: the creative, morally insightful, and visionary sides of it being inherently ordered, the others not. Occasionally in his longer fantasies we sometimes find the protagonists attempting to impart order themselves through explicit commentary on their own behavior; but this is rarely the case with the shorter fairy tales.[17] However, the larger reason for all this stress on order and law is that MacDonald sees the writer creating a little world that mirrors God's own creation of a self-consistent universe.

If fantasies created by the "true" imagination are inherently ordered and "lawful," these laws may be discovered by the sympathetic reader in harmony with the text. Such a reader will be on a journey into the imagination in parallel with the story, penetrating the surface to see the wonderful patterns within. MacDonald may often say that only a child or a mother can truly understand him, that his fairy tales work like aeolian harps or sonatas, arousing hints rather than meanings, or suggesting different meanings to different people, or producing quite different meanings from those intended by their human makers; but in the end he allows that one who diligently looks for the truth will find it: "The man . . . who, in harmony with nature, attempts the discovery of more of her meanings, is just searching out the things of God."[18] We will find that the order and the laws within the tales are often both hidden like God's, and very finely wrought by the imagination of MacDonald. So finely are they wrought, so thoroughly buried within the text that one often has to look long to see them, like telling a partridge from the moorland grass. It is significant that MacDonald often makes keenness of sight a virtue in his fantasy. And such seeing means seeing intuitively, for he finds it particularly in children who see by the light of the imagination.

It has perplexed readers of "The Golden Key" (1867) that the girl Tangle should be treated as inferior to Mossy, and have to go by a much more roundabout route to the same goal, but in fact Mossy sees with his imagination from the first, while Tangle is more the victim of fancy. Early in the story there is a whole series of quasi-moral contrasts made between the two children, hidden behind seemingly innocuous description. Both children,

---

17. Raeper, *George MacDonald*, 313; Zipes, *Fairy Tales and the Art of Subversion*, 104–5, 109.

18. MacDonald, "The Imagination," *A Dish of Orts*, 18.

we are told, live by the forest that fringes Fairyland, but it comes "close up to... [Mossy's] great-aunt's garden and, indeed, sent some straggling trees into it." We learn that Mossy lives with his great aunt beside a fairy wood, listening to stories and reading books; that his father before him found the golden key at the end of the rainbow in Fairyland; and that Mossy is so "keen-sighted" that, helped by the evening sun piercing the wood, he sees the rainbow, of which only the foot is visible, and runs off to reach it. Later he is able to see the Old Man of the Sea in his true form, as Tangle cannot.

Tangle, by contrast, is reared by careless domestics in an untidy house, while her father is frequently away; and her guardians seem to know nothing of Fairyland.[19] Her reading, such as it is, is slow and undirected by any adult, and leaves her a prey to her as yet unruly imagination. Unlike Mossy, she has no motive for gazing at the forest, for nobody has told her of the golden key. She simply lies one evening contentedly looking towards the forest through a window obscured by ivy and other creeping plants; she is driven out of the house by fairies exasperated by its disorder, and chances to run in the direction of the wood.

If Fairyland is equivalent to the imagination, of which the rainbow may also be a symbol, then Mossy is more attuned to it than Tangle. He can see Fairyland as Tangle with her half-obscured window cannot so readily. Indeed, another and lower aspect of the imagination, the tangled worldly consciousness, may rather be said to have made its home in the chaotic and dirty house Tangle inhabits. Mossy leaves his home voluntarily, led by a desire for the golden key: he goes out of his housed and conscious self into the wider imaginative unknown, whereas Tangle is more shut in herself and has to be driven out.

What drives her out gives us insight into the nature of her imagination. We are told that the fairies try in vain to make her leave the house by frightening her with monstrous shapes—apes, carved heads, spider-legged chairs. Tangle does not respond to them because such unnatural things do not inhabit her mind; but the approach of the Three Bears, of which she has just been reading in the fairy story, puts her to flight at once. This shows that while Tangle's imagination is not open to evil images, and contains no tincture of the dark unconscious, it is still subject to delusion.

In the forest Mossy is expected, and the trees and bushes make way for him. Tangle, however, is trapped by a tree dropping its branches around

---

19. See also the shrewd analysis in Kirstin Johnson, "The Progressive Key," 73–74, who amusingly concludes, "Tangle... is a mess."

her, and has to be magically released. When Tangle is taken to a cottage in the wood, a lady there asks her name and age, and has her bathed, tidied, and dressed in new clothes. She gives Tangle a strange fish to eat, whose flesh makes her able to understand the language of the forest animals and insects; and then she has her wait a day until Mossy comes. When Mossy arrives, the lady addresses him by name, and when she sees he has the golden key from the end of the rainbow, serves him and tells him he must go on to find the keyhole that fits the key. No instruction, no corrective bath, and no delay for him; while Tangle is told she should go with him on his journey.

Because Mossy and Tangle are at different stages of imaginative life, they will have different journeys through Fairyland. Though they are at first together, Mossy will later go one way, and Tangle another. For Tangle, we can say, begins in the human unconscious, where Mossy is poised on the verge of the divine imagination. We can go even further, and see Mossy as Tangle's true soul. Because Tangle is more involved (entangled) with this world, her journey towards Mossy's goal must be less self-chosen and more indirect. In fact, after death she must travel through the elements that make up the world. She passes through the bowels of the earth until she ascends inside a mountain. Only by going further down into the mutable elements, from air (and aeranth), down to the water of the ocean, and so down into the earth to the fire, can she find her way to "the land whence the shadows fall." Only by going downwards may she finally ascend. And by "going downwards" may also be meant that she goes back through the earth's history to its beginning in the Oldest Man of All, a baby.[20]

This pattern of descent followed by ascent is caught up in its archetype, as Tangle's journey becomes that of Christ, found by her as a burning child in the fiery depths of the earth. The child gives Tangle a little serpent to guide her to the interior of the mountain. This inverted journey is marked by the three Old Men—of the Sea, the Earth, and the Fire—Tangle meets on the several stages of her descent: each looks increasingly younger, ending in a baby, but the baby is in fact the Oldest Man of all. When Tangle reaches the child, she reaches the heart of heavenly paradox; now a snake, the symbol of evil, will help her to her goal.

This story is not only a pilgrimage through the world to heaven, but also a journey into the imagination to find its divine source. The whole journey is a search for a source, "the country whence the shadows fall," for

---

20. Compare MacDonald, *At the Back of the North Wind*, eds. McGillis and Pennington, where North Wind says the universe may be managed by a baby (85).

a world that has sent its tokens even to the outer margins of the mind, the forest that rims Fairyland and the cottages that rim the soul. As MacDonald puts it,

> To give us the spiritual gift we desire, God may have to begin far back in our spirit, in regions unknown to us, and do much work that we can be aware of only in the results; for our consciousness is to the extent of our being but as the flame of the volcano to the world-gulf whence it issues: in the gulf of our unknown being God works behind our consciousness.[21]

"The Golden Key" can then reveal itself to be about various forms and layers of the imagination, starting with the apparently secular magic of fairy tale, and then moving further within Fairyland and the imagination, through the strange world and the magical beings that uphold it, until one reaches the mystic far country and the divine being at its source, imaged in the burning child that is the Old Man of the Fire. At the end of their journey, when Mossy and Tangle meet again, it is in a room in the heart of a mountain—a room where they find the end of the rainbow and the doorway into it that the golden key unlocks. This is that inmost chamber in the imagination of each man and woman where God lives. As MacDonald says, "God sits in that chamber of our being in which the candle of our understanding goes out in darkness, and sends forth from thence wonderful gifts into the light of that understanding which is His candle."[22] These wonderful gifts are the golden key and the rainbow that will open the way back to the single white radiance from which it came.

Such a deepening journey into the imagination is also implicit in "The Shadows" (1864). Ralph Rinkelmann, on the verge of death, and therefore at one of the most spiritually aware times of his life, is crowned King of Fairy-land by the fairies—or in other terms, he is shown the kingdom of his imagination. His first task is to put down an insurrection by some of the more wicked and ugly of his subjects: that is, he purges his imagination of its more base impulses.[23] Now others of his subjects, the Shadows, are revealed, dancing wildly on the walls of his room/mind. They are at this stage his wild but innocent fancy that riots on the surface of the imagination.

21. MacDonald, *Unspoken Sermons*, 255.
22. MacDonald, "The Imagination," *A Dish of Orts*, 25.
23. Compare also Broome, "Dreams, Fairy Tales, and the Curing of Adela Cathcart," 12, 15, on the unruliness of the shadows as a projection of Rinkelmann's un-integrated self.

But their behavior becomes more sober and steady as Rinkelmann gets to know them and is taken by them to their church in Iceland. There he begins to see how, despite "the insane lawlessness of form in which the Shadows rejoiced," they keep "an identity, each of his own type, inexplicably perceptible through every change" (60). These are the laws that for MacDonald are inherent in the workings of both fancy and imagination when they are part of an invented world.[24] Thereafter Rinkelmann finds that the Shadows in fact operate morally also, to cheer the unhappy, awaken conscience, or expose the wicked. Here the laws that govern their behavior are not individual principles of identity, but universal imperatives. Beyond this, at the very last, Rinkelmann passes beyond spiritual insight to mystic vision. "The shapes had all vanished; and the king, again lifting up his eyes, saw but the wall of his own chamber, on which flickered the Shadow of a Little Child" (79). It is Christmas Day.

In all the tales there is a pattern of breakdown of a settled state, then a period of inversion, followed by a joining of opposites and a new order, which figures the dissolving and remaking of the mind. This is a pattern much like that of comedy, particularly as seen in Shakespeare's comic fantasies *A Midsummer Night's Dream* and *The Tempest*, of which the Victorians were inordinately fond. We start with a motif of separation, with the ogre in "The Giant's Heart" disjoined from his own heart, Little Daylight from her element, the Light Princess from the ground and sense from sense (in the constant puns), or the two children cut off from one another in "The Day Boy and the Night Girl."

The tales are then scattered with pairs of opposites, particularly of day and night, male and female, shadow and substance, nature and civility. This is often accompanied by some kind of wildness—the gambolling shapes in "The Shadows," the fairy fleet that comes down the released stream in "The Carasoyn," the grotesque metamorphoses of the goblin in "Cross Purposes," fancy itself in the Light Princess's absurd condition. Indeed, mobility and metamorphosis become of the essence, and nothing is able to stay the same thing for long. This is highlighted in "Photogen and Nycteris," where the witch's attempts to maintain a constant state of day for the boy and night for the girl are eroded by time and accident.

Then, at the ends of the stories, the enchantment that has produced the initial inversion is itself removed, as a princess recovers her sense of gravity, another princess can live by day as well as night, children are rescued

---

24. MacDonald, "The Fantastic Imagination," *A Dish of Orts*, 314–15.

from the clutches of a giant, and a little girl from the fairies, and two other children at last find their way out of Fairyland. Nearly all the tales have a boy and girl (or a prince and princess) as protagonists, and several end in marriage. And thus these tales, which though called fairy tales are all very different from one another both in character and length, in the end show themselves remarkably alike in their fundamental idiom.

"For the end of imagination is *harmony*,"[25] MacDonald wrote. Evil itself partakes in this process, for the wicked or thieving fairies or the giant bring about an improvement in human spiritual life, while remaining wicked in themselves. "I never knew of any interference on the part of a wicked fairy that did not turn out a good thing in the end," says the narrator in "Little Daylight" (150).[26] Indeed, it can be said that evil is as it is because of some neglect by the "good." It is ugly and distorted partly because it is the ignored or repressed night side of the mind—the imagination itself. Little Daylight is forced to wake only by night because only the sunlight of mental life has been given first place at the palace, from which everything wild has been excluded. In the same way, the witch Watho's action of polarizing day and night in "Photogen and Nycteris" is a symbol of the severance of conscious and unconscious in the minds of men and women. The evil fairies of "Little Daylight" come from the largely unexplored wild wood about the palace, symbolizing the unknown area of mind surrounding the lit and civil one. (In "The Shadows" a special plea is made by the Shadows against the use of artificial light, which banishes darkness.) It is from a similar wood in "The Light Princess" that a prince who will save the princess comes. And in that story, the princess's aunt Makemnoit (the only royal personage named in the whole tale) curses the princess because she has been forgotten[27]—or relegated to the unconscious imagination, and will "make 'em know it."

---

25. MacDonald, "The Imagination," *A Dish of Orts*, 35.

26. Compare the last words of *Phantastes* (1858): "What we call evil, is the only and best shape, which, for the person and his condition at the time, could be assumed by the best good."

27. See also Mendelson, "The Fairy Tales of George MacDonald," 35, "MacDonald makes the evil witch the king's sister, whose dark disposition is really just an aggravated version of his own peevish self-centredness," and "The king's sister (that hidden/neglected part of his heritage)". And Schenkel, "Antigravity," 52–53, seeing the king as cutting himself off from his own unconscious, remarks, "The sister he has forgotten is the right-hand half of his brain, as it were. By refusing the multiplicity and ambivalence of existence he closes himself off against the complexity of mind and soul. Consequently the unconscious punishes him with forgetfulness."

These then are some of the broad recurrent patterns of the tales, but they are considerably refined within each one. Take "The Light Princess" again. Here the banished imagination makes itself felt in hostile form, as an ugly old witch and her curses, which invert the world of sense and reason, and divide words from simple meanings. This is partly symbolized in the two court philosophers consulted for a remedy, Hum-Drum and Kopy-Keck, the one a Materialist, the other a Spiritualist, both following wild hypotheses to find absurd solutions. (Yet by another inversion, both blunder on a more valid suggestion, which is to make the princess cry.) The world of punning is the world of fancy, of "hunting after resemblances that carry with them no interpretation."[28] However, the princess could be said to make a move from fickle fancy towards the deeper imagination when she finds that she regains her physical gravity while swimming in the royal lake, to which she thereafter becomes addicted. Throughout his work MacDonald sees water as a symbol of the imagination, whether the river that floats Anodos deeper into Fairy Land in *Phantastes*, or the stream bringing the fairy fleet into Colin's house in "The Carasoyn," or the frozen Icelandic lake that forms the church of the protagonists in "The Shadows."[29]

Still, though the princess gains her physical gravity and some "sedateness" in the water, she remains otherwise shallow and selfish. When a prince arrives and falls in love with her, she laughs at him, for she does not understand any of the deeper emotions: and at this point the lake begins symbolically to drain away. At the narrative level this has been engineered by her wicked aunt, angry at the princess's ability to circumvent some of the curse: but we also sense that the princess herself has revealed the thinness of her commitment to the imagination. She then has to contemplate the gradual revelation of the muddy bottom the water once covered, "full of lovely creatures dying, and ugly creatures coming to life, like the unmaking of a world" (39). The imagination has exposed itself in monstrous form, as what will in later times be termed the *id*, the very sexuality she has implicitly denied in her mocking treatment of the prince; and her sole desire is now that the lake should be somehow refilled.

For that to happen, the prince must find the hole through which the water has drained and plug it with his own body—a sexual symbol in itself. This necessarily involves his slow drowning, and he makes the princess

---

28. MacDonald, "The Imagination," *A Dish of Orts*, 41.

29. Watkins, "A Theologian's Dealings with the Fairies," 10–12, sees MacDonald as using the symbol of water as "life-giving love" in the fairy tales.

gaze on him as he dies for her (and "dying" here, appropriately enough in a tale concerned with punning, may also carry a sexual meaning).[30] The prince sings to the princess as the water mounts, telling her that without love she would become "'a world that has no well.'" But as foretold, at the prince's death in the deepening lake the princess's shallow fanciful nature leaves her, as she both discovers her love for him and regains her gravity; and this awakened love brings him back to life and her. The formerly hostile aspect of the imagination in the shape of the witch-aunt is destroyed by the very water she released; and in time the lake "wore the roof of the cavern quite through, and was twice as deep as before" (53).

So far we have seen how "The Light Princess" is a picture of the culture of the imagination at a human level—how contact with one's deeper nature is essential to spiritual health. This tale, however, also could be said to show the workings of the imagination from a potentially divine source. As we have seen, MacDonald also maintained that while a man's imagination could shape much of what he wrote, he also might write truths beyond his own knowing, because God was their ultimate author. "A man may well himself discover truth in what he wrote; for he was dealing all the time with things that came from thoughts beyond his own."[31]

It is possible that there is a pattern of Christian symbolism in the story. The evil witch is a form of Satan cast out from heaven, determined to blight God's creation of humanity. When the princess tells the prince that she is "'the only person in my father's kingdom that can't fall!'" (34), we sense she may indeed be fallen in a far deeper sense than mere gravity. The prince, whose love for her leads him to die for her, and so redeem her from the curse, is then a type of Christ,[32] and his journey underground in death (47–48) is at a stretch a harrowing of hell. And his resurrection at the end and marriage of her is apocalyptic, telling of the marriage of Christ and his spiritual bride, the rescued community of mankind. To such depths

---

30. Several critics, starting with Ruskin, have focused on the erotic character of this tale. See, e.g., Wolff, *The Golden Key*, 118, Raeper, *George MacDonald*, 317, Mellon, "The Stages in Adela Cathcart's Cure," 32. Others however stress the moral aspect of development out of narrowness or immaturity: Reis, *George MacDonald's Fiction*, 76–77, Mendelson, "The Fairy Tales of George MacDonald and the Evolution of a Genre," 34–38, Petzold, "Maturation and Education in George MacDonald's Fairy Tales," 19–20.

31. MacDonald, "The Fantastic Imagination," *A Dish of Orts*, 320.

32. See also Raeper, *The Golden Key*, 317 and Mellon, "The Stages in Adela Cathcart's Cure," 32–33. However, while these perceive the action itself as Christ-like, they do not see it as part of a wider spiritual pattern in the tale.

MacDonald's fairy tales can lead us, while still retaining at the surface level of their imagined lakes an air of delightful inconsequence or pleasure in human vagaries.[33]

What then, by contrast, of a simple-seeming story, based on traditional fairy tale motifs, such as "The Giant's Heart" (1863)? In fact, we find that here we have another form of heartlessness, this time embodied in a giant who has put his heart in the care of a savage eagle. As we saw, with its stress on crossing a border into Fairyland, the story points to a move into a world of the imagination, in which giants and hearts in birds' nests are nothing out of the ordinary. In fact, one way of looking at the tale is as a children's nightmare, which is literally punctured by Buffy-Bob at the end when he stabs the heart and kills the giant.[34] At the beginning, the sudden shift of perspective to distortion, as Tricksy-Wee loses her own world and enters that of the giant, conveys this sense of nightmare, as sense-impressions are thrust away by seismic unreality:

> She at length found herself in a valley she knew nothing about. And no wonder; for what she thought was a valley with round, rocky sides, was no other than the space between two of the roots of a great tree that grew on the borders of Giantland. She climbed over the side of it, and went towards what she took for a black, round-topped mountain, far away; but which she soon discovered to be close to her, and to be a hollow place so great that she could not tell what it was hollowed out of. Staring at it, she found it was a doorway.... (81)

There is a similar hallucinatory effect later when Tricksy-Wee "heard a sound like the wind in a tree full of leaves, and could not think what it could be; till, looking up, she found that it was the giantess whispering to her" (82).

It can appear that where in "The Light Princess" there was too little of the imagination, here there is too much, and in a dangerous form. The

---

33. It should be remarked, however, that such an orthodox Christian reading does not express MacDonald's own individual theology, which does not suppose the separate existence of a devil, rejects the idea of all humanity as fallen through a past action, and denies that Christ acted in any magical way as a redeemer of mankind. See Manlove, *Scotland's Forgotten Treasure*, 16–28.

34. Most commentators find the tale too violent, particularly in this ending: but in fact, the end is even crueller in the Norwegian source-tale, "The Giant Who Had No Heart in His Body," where the giant's heart is squeezed inside the duck's egg till he bursts; and this after he has been promised his life for releasing the six brothers he has turned to stone (Dasent, *Popular Tales from the Norse*, 57).

whole tale then becomes the stopping of bad dreams, which are presumably had either by children who eat too much, like Thunderthump's fat captives, or by children who quarrel, like Buffy-Bob and Tricksy-Wee.[35] Such children find themselves discovering a giant country they never knew was there, right next to their own. The image of being eaten by the giant could then refer to their being taken over by bad dreams. Were they to become thin, we learn, Thunderthump would lose interest in them (83). The spiders the children later meet—also frequent inhabitants of nightmare—eat only "'what is mischievous or useless'"(94): this is not just moral, it is psychological—and even psycho-spiritual—in that it says that if you over-eat you become an ogre, and if you are naughty you are made part of a spider.

Reflecting the psychic distortions behind it, "The Giant's Heart" is full of images of separation. It starts by mentioning how "the country of the common people" borders on Giantland, but no one has returned from there to tell about it. Two children of a laborer who lives near the border become parted from one another through a dispute. Then the girl in turn becomes cut off from normal reality when everything—trees, doors, a door knocker, a thimble, and finally a housewife—appears on a gigantic scale. The two children manage to keep apart from those who will be eaten. The giant keeps his heart remote from his body. The children later meet two thrushes, husband and wife, who are at variance, the husband having left the egg-filled nest to please himself. The name of the mountain on which the giant's heart is placed is Skycrack. The eagle who sits on the heart thinking it an egg must be separated from it. The tale also has a motif of lying, of dividing truth from appearance. The giant throws a child in a pot for lying and then lies himself. The children lie to Mrs Thrush about not intending any harm. The giant promises total reform if the children give him back his heart; and then, as they make to do so, tries to destroy them.

For MacDonald, as we saw, "The end of the imagination is *harmony*." The shifting beings of "The Shadows" mutate to spiritual realities. The alienist idiom of "The Giant's Heart" is a distortion of reality that must be corrected through the death of the monstrous giant. The fairies in "Cross Purposes" and "The Carasoyn" have upset the natural order by stealing mortal children, and must be overcome. The witch in "Photogen and Nycteris" has split day and night so that Photogen knows only sunlight, and

---

35. McGillis, *For the Childlike*, 10–11, toys with this point. This is an idea also seen in contemporary fairy tales, such as Annie and E. Keary's "Gladhome" and "Mrs Calkill's Wonderful Underground House" in their *Little Wanderlin and Other Fairy Tales* (1865); or in the celebrated first tale of Christina Rossetti's *Speaking Likenesses* (1874).

Nycteris darkness, until they are brought together. The princess in "Little Daylight" must be restored to the true rhythms of life from which a curse has separated her, and the Light Princess must be returned to both natural law and behavior. This is far too stark a way of putting it, and much amusement is often derived from the particular inversions of nature that have to be corrected: but the idea of recovering harmony underlies all the stories, with the single exception of "The Golden Key," which is not a restoration to a natural state but a transformation into a supernatural one.

"Little Daylight" (1870) is similar in situation and story to "The Light Princess," being about a journey into the imagination, in the shape of a princess who is able to wake only at night and eventually makes her home in the wild woods that surround her father's palace. The narrator begins the story by remarking, "No house of any pretension to be called a palace is in the least worthy of the name, except it has a wood near it—very near it—and the nearer the better." A wandering prince becomes lost in the wood, a double indication of his entering the unconscious. He first sees and falls in love with the princess as a creature of the imagination, dancing and singing. The curse on her can only be lifted by the prince kissing her without knowing it; and this happens when he is looking for her in the dark of the moon and comes across a wretched woman whom he kisses for very charity, only to find the princess standing before him. The emphasis on not knowing concerns living in the imagination. But the imagination itself is not all good, for it is the realm both of creative and destructive impulses; the prince has overcome the latter by kissing the princess through innocent charity rather than desire.[36]

But the story is more complex than this. The princess's name is Little Daylight, and when the prince saves her he restores her to the day and to waking life. The tale is trying to say that just as we need to live in the darkness of the imagination, so we need also to inhabit the sister world of the sun and the more conscious mind. Of this latter aspect of mind the civilized court to which the two return is a symbol; so too is the emphasis throughout on the laws governing fairy curses and blessings alike, so that both come to pass. And within the wood the prince is directed by another figure of order and control, in the shape of the old fairy woman with whom he sojourns. Just as the prince in "The Light Princess" goes into the depths so that the princess may live aright in the world, so here the prince goes into

---

36. It will be seen that the plot and setting of this story have many similarities to Shakespeare's *A Midsummer Night's Dream*.

the dark so that she may come into the light. It must be admitted however that this theme is rather more a postulated than a lived truth, since most of the story is set in the forest and at night, without reference to the court or the sun. MacDonald is on the whole more interested in moonlight, darkness, and night.

"Photogen and Nycteris" (1879) describes an experiment by the witch Watho (Know-Nothing?) to cut a boy off from knowledge of the night and a girl from the day. This fails when both children come together and begin to share their different lives. The whole tale is an image of the mind divided, the unconscious imagination kept forgotten in the dark, and the surface mind of daily life in the light; and the witch is an extreme symbol of this polarizing habit. Without links to a deeper self, Photogen is shallow and selfish, while, with knowledge only of the dark, lamp-lit world within, Nycteris continually misinterprets the outer one. The one terrified of night, the other of day, the one empirical and outward-looking, the other inward and imaginative, each is confounded when it meets its opposite. But the synthesis of the two destroys the analytic experiment of the witch, who turns to a furious wolf and is then self-killed by an arrow. One recalls MacDonald's remark, "Analysis is well, as death is well; analysis is death, not life."[37] Like others of the fairy tales, this story points to a dangerous separation of man from his imagination that MacDonald seems to have felt was a modern disease; for it is one of his central and most distinctive themes.

The issues in the remaining tales "Cross Purposes" (1862) and "The Carasoyn" (1866) are a little different. Here the concern is mainly with the imagination as possible illusion or deceit. So taken is Colin by the fairy queen in "The Carasoyn" that he falls into the trap of agreeing to do what she asks in order to rescue the little captive girl she has, and is told to carry out a humanly impossible task. This, and his meeting with the fairies while he is asleep, is a way of conveying Colin's entry into the world of the imagination. Indeed, the girl called Fairy that he wants is herself a symbol of the enchanted mind. Colin now remembers how once when he was lost on the moor he met a wise old woman: so he contrives to lose himself again, that is, go further into the imagination; and indeed then he meets her and is told what he must do to gain the bottle of Carasoyn. The tasks all involve the imagination—he must "'dream three days without sleeping . . . [then] work three days without dreaming . . . [then] work and dream three days together'" (197). And during all of these Colin is to be unaware that he is

---

37. MacDonald, *Unspoken Sermons*, 464.

carrying them out. The tasks he meanwhile performs seem absurd—to help the dwarfs "'lift Cumberbone Crag a yard higher, and send a flue under Stonestarvit Moss'" (199). He is having to live through the seemingly nonsensical and disconnected imaginative world that is the realm of the fairies themselves, in order to secure the fairy child. And even when that is done the fairy queen tries to deceive him once more, when the child she yields him is turned to a variety of beasts that would have escaped Colin had he not held on to them. But the larger illusion is suffered by the fairy queen herself, for the Carasoyn she has so desired makes her and her people suddenly old and wretched when they have it, and they have to leave that part of the country.

The continuation MacDonald added to this tale in 1867 is, like "Little Daylight" in relation to "The Light Princess," something of a repetition. Where Colin ended by winning back and then marrying a girl child, the fairies here begin by stealing his own boy child by her, and he must visit the old woman again to find out what he must do. This ends with him making a circle about the fairies as he did around the Carasoyn, and with the fairy queen again trying to deceive him with false versions of the child. Here much more is done for him by the old woman of the moor, and he does not have to work for the creatures from whom he obtains the objects to defeat the fairies: we are to assume that, now an initiate of the imagination, Colin is more directly helped by its better denizens. But there is a larger irony, and that is that in this story Colin is a victim of his own illusion, for he believes that in moving to Devonshire, where this story is set, he will escape the fairies of his earlier experience—only to find that he has chosen precisely the place to which they themselves have moved. This apparent coincidence suggests that the fairies are more a part of Colin than he will admit. They can be seen partly as his own distorted imagination, which will not run true until he has rescued from fairy perversion the true forms of both his child-wife and their child.

In "Cross Purposes" illusion is the central topic. The squire's daughter Alice has a penchant for the prettified imagination, and appropriately is drawn into Fairyland by the "aesthetic" fairy Peaseblossom, through a swooning landscape of beautiful flowers, limpid pools, and moonlight, where "Any flower she wished to see she had only to wish for, and she was sure to find it" (105). Poor and solitary boy Richard is also readily pulled, "laughing and following" (108), towards Fairyland, but here by a much more active and comic imagination in the form of the shape-shifting goblin

Toadstool.[38] Alice's passive imagination renders her helpless when she is abandoned in Fairyland, but Richard's more self-aware and educated faculty (he reads more books) enables him to take charge and penetrate the frauds and shows of Fairyland to find a way out of it for them both.

It is Richard who opposes the fairies' intention to take them to their court, at which the children are abruptly abandoned by their guides. It is clear that Richard has more connection with the outside world. When we meet him first, he has saved up to buy his mother an umbrella, he is looking round the market, and his "fairy" Toadstool's changes are of common things, from umbrellas to geese and mushrooms. So it is that Colin sees through all the deceptive appearances Fairyland presents as he and Alice try to leave it—the seemingly deep water across a passage, the cat that turns into an apparent mountain, the great heights of buildings that turn out to be within a step of the ground. Meanwhile Fairyland, which for Alice was previously a pretty place, devoid of "mud, or frogs, or water-lizards, or eels" (105), becomes crowded with them on the children's journey back—but that too is an illusion, for as soon as Richard jumps among them, they disappear. Under Richard's guidance Alice too has come to realize something of the deceptive power of Fairyland and of her own self-pleasing imagination.

At the end Toadstool and Peaseblossom are banished from the fairy court for what they did, and "The Fairy Queen sent . . . [the children] permission to visit Fairyland as often as they pleased; and no goblin or fairy was allowed to interfere with them." This represents both the purification of the imagination, and the fact that the children are no longer at the mercy of their illusions, and can enter and leave their inner worlds freely.

Taken together, MacDonald's fairy tales are a series of different journeys, each with its own human starting point, into that faculty whose culture he felt to be the key to life. Sometimes the journey leads to illusion, sometimes to nightmare, sometimes to mystic vision; it may express the inner natures of the travellers, or it may take them out of themselves to a reality beyond them. It may be circular, returning to where it started from, restoring a princess to her gravity or another to daylight, or simply getting back home again. Or it may be linear, moving to ever-deeper experience like that of Ralph Rinkelmann in "The Shadows," or else breaking out into a new reality, as in "The Golden Key." The world it enters may be wider

---

38. A. Waller Hastings, "Social Conscience and Class Relations in MacDonald's 'Cross Purposes,'" 81–82, puts the contrasting fairies in terms of the class difference between Alice and Richard.

than our own, or it may be narrower and more constrained, as in the curses laid on the two princesses or the confinements of Photogen and Nycteris. Where it is dark, or narrow, or illusive, that is through some human failure which has stunted its proper growth, and this is put right through the removal of some curse or an escape from some prison. "Man's occupation with himself turns his eyes from the great life beyond his threshold."[39] So, while these tales show both right and wrong uses of the imagination, they all enjoin that we enter it. MacDonald wrote, "Seek not that your sons and your daughters should not see visions, should not dream dreams; seek that they should see true visions, that they should dream noble dreams."[40]

---

39. MacDonald, "A Sketch of Individual Development" (1880), *A Dish of Orts*, 54.
40. MacDonald, "The Imagination," *A Dish of Orts*, 30.

3

At the Back of the North Wind (1870)

The Imagination in the World

The longer children's fantasies by MacDonald that follow the fairy tales are more consistent in nature. All of them tend to the visionary end of the spectrum embodied in "The Golden Key." They deal with the imagination that concerns itself with realities rather than illusions, fictions, or games of logic. Their imagery is dipped in the numinous. All of them have at their centres great and mystical female figures, guiding the human protagonists on their adventures. These are, more and less, embodiments of the divine imagination. Some have called them the *anima*, or Sophia, but in the holy faculty of the imagination they have their being, and all mortals who relate to them truly have made that faculty and all that it supernaturally portends their home.

In MacDonald's shorter fairy tales we never leave some form of the imagination, and we are always in a fantastic world. But in all MacDonald's longer children's fantasy, the world of the imagination embodied in these great female figures is not the only one, and is under continual challenge, whether by bleak everyday fact, by reason, by obdurate evil, by empiricism, or by self love. And in one fantasy it is placed beside another world that does not recognize its existence. That fantasy is *At the Back of the North Wind*.

George MacDonald's Children's Fantasies and the Divine Imagination

At the Back of the North Wind was serialized in *Good Words for the Young* from October 1868 to November 1870, then under MacDonald's editorship. It tells of the boy Diamond's life as a cab-man's son in a poor area of mid-Victorian London, and of his meetings and adventures with a lady called North Wind; and it includes the separate fairy-tale "Little Daylight," two dream-stories, and several long poems. Generally well received by the public, it has hardly been out of print since.

This is MacDonald's only fantasy set mainly in this world. In *Phantastes* (1858), Anodos goes into Fairy Land and in *Lilith* Mr Vane finds himself in the "region of the seven dimensions." In the later "Princess" books we are in a fairy-tale realm of kings, princesses, and goblins; and the worlds of the shorter fairy tales are all full of fairies, witches, and giants. But Diamond's story nearly all happens either in Victorian London or in other parts of the world where North Wind takes him. By weaving together these two contexts, the one urban, the other natural, MacDonald is trying to show how both ordinary human life and the elemental forces of this world are joined in God.

Indeed, the outer world and its foundations are much more the topic in this book than in MacDonald's other fantasies, which are often more concerned with personal issues and inner landscapes. Of course, since for MacDonald the outer world is also a figure of the inner one, the two are not finally separate: "All that moves in the mind is symbolized in Nature."[1] But it is a question of emphasis. Where in his other stories the protagonists go from an inner world, often a house, to impact on a world outside, in *At the Back of the North Wind* the outside world initially breaks in on an inner one. The book starts with the North Wind blowing away a patch from Diamond's thin bedroom wall to pierce through and force him out of bed to meet her outside. Thereafter she often enters his childhood life, taking him on trips with her that culminate in a journey to a country she says is at her back, and which is probably the picture of an antechamber to heaven.

Thus, while the immediate reality of the book is the world of everyday Victorian lower-class London, which appears to most of its inhabitants to have nothing supernatural about it, this is mixed with the appearance of a mystical lady who claims to be the north wind. Then too there is little Diamond himself, who seems exceptionally innocent for his milieu. Later this same Diamond becomes wise and spiritually insightful far beyond his years. During the story Diamond has a dream, which could be real, about

---

1. MacDonald, "The Imagination," *A Dish of Orts*, 9.

some star children who are angels. There is also a talking horse called Ruby who is a horse-angel, sent to try Diamond's father.

However, all these supernatural beings and events are also as seen by a child when asleep, or sick, or to outsiders deranged. They are allowed to be the products of a mind, at the same time that we are asked to believe them real. They are seen by the imagination, which at the same time as being capable of delusion was, for MacDonald, the means of perceiving a deeper world than our eyes can see working through our own. That ambiguity is at the heart of *At the Back of the North Wind*.[2]

In *At the Back of the North Wind*, MacDonald brings together the idiom of the novels of "real life" he had been writing since *David Elginbrod* (1864) with the remoter-seeming worlds of his fantasy stories. Two of the novels written at the time of *At the Back of the North Wind*—*Robert Falconer* (1867) and *Guild Court* (1868)—concerned the miseries and temptations of London life and the need for Christian faith to look beyond them. Now MacDonald tries to show that for those who have eyes to see—and for him that usually means children and some mothers—the world is full of ultimately benign supernatural forces that control its workings.

The book is less a story with a central plot than an episodic spiritual biography. It falls into two parts, the first third of it being the series of adventures Diamond has with North Wind, and the remainder mainly describing his time as a replacement cab driver for his sick father. In the second part, Diamond is more a boy than a child, and North Wind does not visit him until he is dying. (There is ambiguity here as to whether North Wind takes him while he is terminally ill, or when he is spiritually ripe.) Throughout the book, Diamond is learning about the nature of this world and of the world behind the North Wind that comes after it. At the same time he becomes more and more a worker for good in his community, to the growing wonder of all about him.

---

2. David S. Robb, *George MacDonald*, 124–25, says, "The reality of what is happening to Diamond is only very occasionally, and indirectly, glimpsed . . . and the positive side of his fate is given priority. . . . Even the open windows which kill him (the knot-hole in the thin partition at the beginning; the open bedroom window by which he waits for North Wind for the last time) are made to seem natural and positive things, with scarce a hint of the danger which, from the mortal perspective, they represent." Robb sees this as a strategy by which MacDonald attempts "to transform our vision of death, and to offer it as something to be wholeheartedly accepted, despite understandable mortal doubts." While this is certainly true, it is also the case that MacDonald seeks to blur causality to further his vision of a universe at once mysterious and incoherent.

MacDonald wrote *At the Back of the North Wind* partly in response to Charles Kingsley's *The Water-Babies: A Fairy Tale for a Land-Baby* (1863).[3] Kingsley's submarine world in *The Water-Babies* is presented as a reality, in which a Yorkshire chimney-sweep's boy Tom, who runs away from his employment over the moors, falls into a stream and turns into a water-baby, before swimming down to the sea and finding out all about how the world is run. There he meets the great fairies Mrs Doasyouwouldbedoneby and Mrs Bedonebyasyoudid, who represent the laws of action and reaction, both physical and moral, in the world; and in the Arctic, on his way to the Other-end-of-Nowhere, he encounters Mother Carey, the generative principle, who makes creatures make themselves. At the end, Tom has a vision in which all these great fairies come together into one "who was neither of them, and yet all of them at once," and whose true name shines so intensely from her eyes that Tom cannot read it.

So too in *At the Back of the North Wind* young Diamond meets the great fairy North Wind, who apart from being a natural force is also a moral one, waking the evil to a sense of their wicked ways, sometimes operating as a special providence to produce happy outcomes, sometimes engineering disasters that she believes will do good beyond her knowledge. Like Kingsley's fairies, North Wind's actions are directed by a larger power; but unlike them she is under immediate orders, whereas they are "wound up" from the beginning of time to work like machines.[4] As for MacDonald's hero young Diamond, he travels like Kingsley's Tom to the Arctic to find a strange land; and like Tom he meets on the ice the motionless figure of a seated woman—for him North Wind, for Tom Mother Carey, who makes all creatures "'make themselves.'"[5] Both Tom and Diamond experience a steadily widening world.

Kingsley intended his book to counter the materialist implications of Charles Darwin's *Origin of Species* (1859), then causing much consternation among believers. He said that the aim of *The Water-Babies* was to show to all sorts of unbelieving people that "there is a quite miraculous and divine element underlying all physical nature."[6] MacDonald's story may itself be an attempt, like Kingsley's, to answer the implications of Darwin's views—

3. See Manlove, "MacDonald and Kingsley," 140–62.
4. Kingsley, *The Water-Babies*, 220.
5. Kingsley, *The Water-Babies*, 307.
6. Letter of summer 1862 in Frances E. Kingsley, ed., *Charles Kingsley, Letters and Memories of his Life*, vol. 2, 137.

namely, that the universe is merely the physical setting for the working out of the natural laws of selection. Although MacDonald hardly ever refers to Darwin in his work, as a trained scientist he would have been deeply interested in his ideas, and keen to deny their purely physical view of the world. And he often maintained that the imagination could find out the deep things of the world as reason and empirical science could not.[7]

While Kingsley and MacDonald both see the universe as created by God, their views of the relation of God to nature are quite different. Kingsley, following William Paley's *Natural Theology* (1802), sees the world as a perfectly comprehensible machine with a discoverable maker at its root. For MacDonald, the world is rather a network of relationships shot through with mystery. MacDonald believed that no intelligence of man could find out God,[8] and that the kind of definiteness and certainty that Kingsley sought was quite untrue to the nature of the world. For MacDonald, the universe is the living imagination of God at work, and it can only be approached through the imagination—whether in dreams, fairy tales, or visions. Above all, it can only be understood by sympathy, by involvement in it, not by standing back and analyzing it.

Indeed, *At the Back of the North Wind* can be said to be founded on uncertainties. Diamond and his mystical experiences are set not in an fairyland but in a disbelieving urban world where the concern of people to scrape a living takes up almost all their time and any thing that is not physical and immediate is largely irrelevant. MacDonald gives us freedom to ask whether Diamond is deluded about North Wind, and whether the harsh reality of the life around him is the only truth. His answer is that Diamond's vision is both a dream and a reality.

On the side of its being all "only" a dream, Diamond is a child, that is, someone not yet sure of the boundaries of reality. Then, North Wind has to obey "'the law about the children'" and come to Diamond only when he is asleep in bed (47–52, 65, 89–90, 113–14).[9] Though Diamond twice meets her outside, this is when he is sitting down, drowsy or tired and hot (82–83, 111–12), and then North Wind does not take him, only talks to him. Then there is the fact that Diamond is sometimes said to be ill, suggesting that his

---

7. MacDonald, "The Imagination," *A Dish of Orts*, 28.

8. "No wisdom of the wise can find out God.... The simplicity of the whole natural relation is too deep for the philosopher" (MacDonald, *The Hope of the Gospel and the Miracles of Our Lord*, 153–54; see also 58.

9. References are to MacDonald, *At the Back of the North Wind*, eds. McGillis and Pennington.

vision of North Wind might be a feverish dream. Finally, there is the view of most people about Diamond, that his supposed adventures with North Wind are a sign of mental instability: his down-to-earth friend Nanny says he "'must ha' got out o' one o' them Hidget Asylums'"(78) and that he has "'a tile loose'" (172); the cab drivers call him "'God's baby'" and his mother is often alarmed when he starts talking about the country at North Wind's back.

But if there is much suggestion that North Wind is a dream, there is at the same time clear evidence that Diamond "really" went with her. Nanny, the crossing sweeper from another part of London, remembers him later, and he could not otherwise have known about the ship North Wind sank that had Miss Coleman's lover on it. Nor, illiterate as he was, could he have known anything of how the wind works on a ship or about the different freighters that go north towards the Arctic. And mentioned above, while it is true that Diamond is sometimes ill after he has been with North Wind, allowing for her having been a dream born of sickness, his being ill is not always clear; and sometimes he seems perfectly well after she has come, as on the first two occasions when he is left outside in a freezing garden and then in the windswept London streets. And, we might add, it would not be too surprising if he were ill after really meeting North Wind, since she takes him out into the cold in his nightgown. While North Wind may be an illusion, she is no less possibly a reality.

As for Diamond's being "only a child" when he has his visions, MacDonald would turn that on its head by saying that it is only to the child that God sends true visions. Only the pure child like Diamond can be the aeolian harp on which North Wind can play God's music. For the true divine universe, the universe that MacDonald describes as a wondrous, dreamlike fairy tale, is rarely glimpsed by adults. Only a pure child like Diamond can meet the wild North Wind; only he can see something of how the world truly works, only he can have a vision of the country at the back of the North Wind. God "can be revealed only to the child; perfectly, to the pure child only. All the discipline of the world is to make men children, that God may be revealed to them."[10]

In the first third of the story Diamond is a child and sees North Wind often, but she does not come to him when he has grown to a boy and becomes a more active member of his community. North Wind is still about, managing certain events behind the scenes (132–33, 164, 213–14, 216,

---

10. MacDonald, *The Hope of the Gospel and the Miracles of Our Lord*, 153.

242–44, 252, 256), but Diamond does not see her. He believes in her just as much, but she is not so directly a part of his life.

The issue concerning North Wind's reality comes to a head at the end of the story when Diamond, perhaps worn down by others' disbelief, perhaps sensing the approach of his own death (which North Wind partly represents), asks her whether she is indeed real. She has no way of proving her reality to him, and also says that the way she appears to Diamond is not the form she uses with less innocent people. She suggests that if she were only a dream, Diamond could not have loved her as a real person; and even then, "'I don't think you could dream anything that hadn't something real like it somewhere'" (288). At the end however, Diamond says, "'I can't feel quite sure yet'"; to which North Wind replies, "'You must wait a while for that. Meantime you may be hopeful, and content not to be quite sure'" (290). And we too are left, still having to see North Wind as both a truth and as an illusion.

But MacDonald would maintain that this uncertainty is the best state, because it is most true to the nature of the God-created universe we inhabit. Fantasy, which of its very nature invites disbelief, can actually be the sole means of awakening it. Fantasy is like dreaming and imagining, but dreams can come from the deepest truth. As Anodos puts it at the end of *Phantastes*, "When a man dreams his own dream, he is the sport of his dream; when Another gives it him, that Other is able to fulfil it."

It is a more mystical, even sacramental, universe that *At the Back of the North Wind* tries to portray. However much it seems corroded by bad human choices, this world is still potentially the one that God created and continually thinks into being.[11] In this world of the divine imagination, every human being and environment may be a thought in the mind of God. In such a world there will be nowhere without God—"it is not, could not, be."[12] Seen in this way the whole story is carried forward within the imagination of God. In this sense, ideally read, it is a continuous mystical experience. Indeed, MacDonald says, "I believe that every fact in nature is a revelation of God."[13]

But such an understanding of the world or the book is not to be made by rational means, only through trusting relationship with God. This is not so abstract as it seems, but is rather a matter of induced feeling. Like others

---

11. MacDonald, *George MacDonald in the Pulpit*, 106.
12. MacDonald, *Unspoken Sermons*, 611.
13. MacDonald, *Unspoken Sermons*, 463.

of MacDonald's fantasies, particularly *Phantastes* and *Lilith, At the Back of the North Wind* asks for a non-conscious response to the story, because only that way will we intuit rather than try to be certain of its meaning. Unlike in *Phantastes* and *Lilith,* the way to this is through love. In *At the Back of the North Wind* we have two loving characters at the center. In this story MacDonald wants to break down our way of reducing life and art to schemes and patterns, and to respond at a much more intimate level. For him, the discovered meaning of a story can get in the way of its being. That is why he writes the book for young children, who for him put few structures between themselves and direct experience.

> To reveal is immeasurably more than to represent; it is to present to the eyes that know the truth when they see it[;] . . . to see God and to love him are one. He can be revealed only to the child; perfectly, to the pure child only. All the discipline of the world is to make men children, that God may be revealed to them.[14]

A child's eye can see the world directly and for itself, without connecting things together with the intellect and so distancing them. Moreover, everything is seen as strange, so that a lady called North Wind breaking into Diamond's sleep at night is not much odder to him than having the family horse stabled downstairs, or a poet in a rowing boat. It is just our habit of making connections among things, rather than regarding them for themselves, that MacDonald wants to remove, so that we can perceive the world not only as wonderful but also as a miracle continually being worked by God. Charles Kingsley in *The Water-Babies* might prove the existence of God at work in nature by an analytic process going literally deeper, from stream to river to sea to ocean, but for MacDonald, God is not to be proved from a distance and by a logical sequence, but experienced immediately through his creation, in something like, but also more than, Gertrude Stein's "A rose is a rose is a rose." MacDonald writes that "the truth of a flower" is "not the facts about it, be they correct as ideal science itself, but the shining, glowing, patient thing throned on its stalk." For the flower is "a perfect thought from the heart of God—a truth of God!—not an intellectual truth, but a divine fact"; and thus "The truth *of a thing* . . . is the blossom of it, the thing it is made for, the topmost stone set on with rejoicing."[15]

---

14. MacDonald, "The Imagination," *A Dish of Orts*, 30.
15. MacDonald, *Unspoken Sermons*, 465, 467, 469.

At the Back of the North Wind (1870)

At the Back of the North Wind is written in defiance of logical or narrative connections that give us certainties that are not to be had. It will not give us a clear story, or a fictional microcosm that is inviolate, or a person whose nature is clear, or a statement that is not somewhere contradicted. It is written to remove such false links with the world of the book so that the true ones may be revealed. This story is continually subversive. But also, in breaking down of ordinary linkages between things, MacDonald shows the deeper mystical links between things that only a God-inspired imagination can perceive.

This is seen from the outset. An "I" narrator tells us enigmatically that he has been asked to write about the country at the back of the North Wind. He mentions an account by the Greek historian Herodotus of a people called Hyperboreans who lived there and found it so pleasant that they drowned themselves. But then he says he is not going to tell that story because Herodotus did not have the right account of the place. In fact, "I am going to tell you how it fared with a boy who went there." We wonder who has asked this narrator to write about the other country Diamond visits, and why. Then all his statements seem rather ill-fitting. He introduces Herodotus only to set him aside. He tells us of a people who killed themselves because they were "so comfortable." And in the end it seems he is not going to tell us about the country so much as about "how it fared with a boy who went there." It seems difficult to speak precisely.

In the next paragraph the narrator sets a scene that is the reverse of comfortable. He says his boy hero lived in a room above a coach house, but he describes no more of this room than one thin and rotten wall against which the north wind blows. Then he says,

> Still, this room was not very cold, except when the north wind blew stronger than usual: the room I have to do with now was always cold, except in summer, when the sun took the matter into his own hands. Indeed I am not sure whether I ought to call it a room at all; for it was just a loft where they kept hay and straw and oats for the horses. And when little Diamond . . . But stop: I must tell you that his father, who was a coachman, had named him after a favourite horse, and his mother had had no objection:—when little Diamond, then, lay there in bed, he could hear the horses under him munching away in the dark . . . .

We are told how biting the wind was against the thin wall; then that the room within was not usually so cold at all; then that there is another room that is to be our main concern; then that this non-located room is not properly a room at all. The narrator tells us it is always cold, and then retracts, "except in summer." When he starts to describe this last place he happens on little Diamond, who could as well be a horse as a boy (which in fact is true), and then veers off to tell us how he got his name and what his mother thought of it. He uses orotund phrases, "took the matter into his own hands," "had no objection." In and out of this ill-fitting assemblage of rambling statements details gleam, "always cold, except in summer," "where they kept hay and straw and oats for the horses," "he could hear the horses under him." Everything no sooner is, than in a sense it is not, and slips from our grasp. Nothing is articulated without a qualification. And in fact this sense of things slipping out of reach is characteristic of the reader's experience of the book as a whole.

For, just as the wind is changeable, often abruptly, so is the story. No sooner are we given a sequence of events than it is gone, and the other way round. In the first part of the book North Wind comes to Diamond only at odd intervals. As the wind, we suppose, she is variable; and as a child, so is he. She visits him first when he is asleep, and tells him to get up and follow her, but he stops to stroke the horse Diamond in the stall under his room, and when he goes out she is gone—although a cold wind blows him along a path and through a door into the next-door garden of his father's employers, the Colemans. He is seen in the garden by the Colemans' old nurse, and taken in and returned home. Immediately he wakes up, he hears the horse moving below, and goes down and gets into difficulties climbing onto his back. This series of changing directions has all the randomness of life or of North Wind herself, but little of the purpose of a story.

Thereafter Diamond is kept indoors for some days and we watch him play. Then he is allowed out; and shortly after that, North Wind comes back to him again at night and takes him flying with her over London, in her work of sweeping the streets with her "'great besom'" (72). But when Diamond sees a little girl being blown about by her, he asks to be set down to help her. So that abruptly ends that contact too, and we are back with the "real" world again. Again we follow Diamond's everyday life for some time; until, a few months later, he finds North Wind in the garden next door, chasing a sleepy bee out of a tulip. They talk together, until Diamond finds that she has gone. And so it goes on. We do not know why North Wind has attached herself to Diamond; what she does often seems inconsequential; we can never settle with her before she is away; and we are kept flickering between outings with her and Diamond's daily family life. North Wind's visits to Diamond are like Novalis's picture of the fairy tale as an aeolian harp, a harp that sounds as the random wind blows through it (from the epigraph to MacDonald's *Phantastes*, 1858).

After Diamond returns from the country at North Wind's back and she largely disappears from the story, we enter on an entirely new prospect concerning his later boyhood in London, and the changing fortunes of his family. We have moved away from night to day, and from the world of the mind to one that is much more of the body and its needs—cab driving that moves people about, houses for shelter and security, hospitals for sick children, babies to be fed and cleaned, men who beat their wives. Diamond's father loses his job after his employers, the Colemans, are ruined, and the family move to Bloomsbury; Diamond then helps at home with the new baby, learns how to drive a cab, is taught to read, takes over the cab driving from his father when the latter falls ill, and supports the family. Then his father's fortunes change for the better and he is made coachman to Mr Raymond at his country house. This part of the book is more a story of a boyhood in Victorian London, of everyday life on the edge of poverty, of chances that help and accidents that hinder, and of good acts occasionally rewarded. The randomness of the story is now coming as much from its realism as its fantasy, which begins to convey to us the idea that our world may be no less fantastic than what we call fantasy itself.

Yet this part of the book is less a continuous story than a sequence of vignettes, for it is still continually interrupted by fantastic episodes, poems and stories—a visionary experience Diamond has with some star-children, a long fairy story, "Little Daylight," a dream of Nanny's about visiting the Man in the Moon, a conversation between two horses, one of which is an angel in disguise, a long poem, and numerous nursery rhymes. Every one of these "interpolations" is mysterious, and has no explanation or interpretation. Just as in the first part of the book, we are still being switched continually between Victorian reality and fantasy, suggesting that there are finally no walls between them. Reality is not single but multiple: it is not realism *or*, but realism *and* fantasy together.

Few links in the story are those of cause and effect. North Wind comes to Diamond by seeming chance. Chance impoverishes the Colemans and forces Diamond's father to look for new work. Chance makes him ill and makes Diamond a young cab driver. Chance makes Diamond ill; chance makes him die. Dreams and stories come and go randomly. But seen more deeply, chance is part of a holy plan we cannot fathom: "All luck is good."[16]

In the view of the critic John Pennington, *At the Back of the North Wind* is metafictional, reacting in part against the positivism of the realistic novel that dominated mid-Victorian fiction, and that formed a large part of MacDonald's own literary output. "By dislocating structure through metafictional means . . . MacDonald blurs the distinction between reality and fantasy and suggests that fantasy is also reality or another form of reality." From the metafictional point of view, "reality" is no less of a construct than fantasy: but Pennington locates a fundamental and unaltered reality beyond our existence, the world at North Wind's back. When he says that in *At the Back of the North Wind* MacDonald "challenges the reader's narrative assumptions, breaks them, and provides the reader with a higher reality—death," the implicit idea here of a real world and fantasy married in a fantastic reality that transcends them is one that replaces the subversions of metafictional discourse with the idealistic certainties of Fichtean dialectic.[17] For the plain fact is that at the end of the story the whole notion of the reality of North Wind and of a higher reality beyond her is subjected to intense questioning. And it is the strength of *At the Back of the North Wind* that this should be so, and that while heaven is the ultimate reality wished for, and potentially the immutable truth beyond all our fictions, its possible non-existence is so squarely faced. This is part of God's dealings with us through the world, that he appears *both* present *and* absent. Beyond that we cannot have certainty unless we commit ourselves to belief; and, this side of death, even that belief is still no more than belief.

God is, and God is not; Diamond's visions are both true and false; the world is just and the world is unjust. It is not a question of either/or in this story but of both/and. We at once believe and disbelieve in Diamond's visions; we both accept and reject North Wind's words of comfort. That is, we live in continual contradiction, now accepting one side more, now less. Diamond shows us the way forward, through love and continual faith, if only we can follow. But following Diamond will not give certainty one way or the other. When last we see him he is still in doubt as to the reality of his supernatural experiences; and not one of his own people has followed his example. Only the pressure of the book in which he features makes us incline, like the bourgeois sympathizers at the end, to believe his story true.

16   Williams, "The Death of Good Fortune," *Collected Plays*, 179, 192.

17.   Pennington, "Alice at the Back of the North Wind," 54–56.

But then it is true only within a book which, however divinely inspired, is still a fiction.

Adding to the general uncertainty is the fact that, alone of all the great female figures in MacDonald's fantasies, North Wind is not omniscient. She says she is only the agent of a greater power whose purposes she does not fully understand. Often when she is consoling Diamond, she is also trying to reassure herself. Nor is she in the position of authority that all the other great ladies have. Irene's grandmother is the wellspring of spiritual truth in the "Princess" books, the wise woman is the arbiter of the moral fates of Rosamond and Agnes in *The Lost Princess*, but North Wind has been left to fend for herself as a force of nature, with only "a far-off song" to reassure her (97). Even Kingsley's fairy Mrs Bedonebyasyoudid, North Wind's natural equivalent in *The Water-Babies*, is more confident of her role: "'I never was made, my child; and I shall go on for ever and ever; for I am as old as Eternity, and yet as young as Time.'"[18] But North Wind can only say, "'I don't know. I obeyed orders'"(113). In *At the Back of the North Wind* MacDonald has dared to do without an authority figure who gives us certainties.

North Wind says she loves Diamond and yet she can sink a ship full of innocent people in a storm. When asked why by Diamond she says she does not know why she does it. But she claims it is all done for love, because if Diamond loves the self or "me" that he knows her to be, she must still be the same loveable person when she does harsh-seeming things, or else "'there would be two mes'" (93). To the childlike she will appear beautiful, but to those doing wrong or in need of violent change, even death, she may appear as a wolf or a storm: "'I have to shape myself various ways to various people. But the heart of me is true'" (289).

Later she adds that she can bear to sink the ship because she hears a universal song coming nearer in which all the cries of the drowning people are caught up and transformed into joy. To which,

> "But that won't do them any good—the people, I mean," persisted Diamond.
>
> "It must. It must," said North Wind hurriedly. "It wouldn't be the song it seems to be if it did not swallow up all their fear and pain too, and set them singing it themselves with all the rest. I am sure it will." (63)

---

18. Kingsley, *The Water-Babies*, 221.

When "doubting little Diamond" learns from North Wind that although the ship was sunk, she saved a few people who reached a desert island, he asks, "'And what good will come of that?'" to which she can only reply with her "'I don't know. I obeyed orders'"(113).

At one point North Wind turns the tables on Diamond and suggests that the real "she" might not be the kind one he knows but the cruel one that sinks the ship, the kind one being only a pretence: at which Diamond clings to her crying,

> "No, no, dear North Wind; I can't believe that. I don't believe it. I won't believe it. That would kill me. I love you, and you must love me, else how did I come to love you? How could you know how to put on such a beautiful face if you did not love me and the rest? No. You may sink as many ships as you like, and I won't say another word." (94)

Even this argument is but a straw in the Wind herself. It is the logic of a child who has never met or even fallen in love with a beauty who is evil—a wicked flirt, a temptress, a Lilith. All arguments are, for MacDonald, helpless to prove either the existence or the nature of God. We cannot finally be certain which kind of being North Wind is, and her two selves remain as irreconcilable to mortals as their sufferings at the hands of a supposedly loving God. An interpretation of this book that said that North Wind was a form of the devil tempting Diamond as Christ, and bringing him to eventual ruin could not be disproved. Certainly, "nice kind lady" aside, North Wind must remain a problematic, Janus-like figure to our intellects, for it is only through faith and love that one can feel and trust in her essential goodness.

Throughout the book we are made unsure of the identities of things. Is a book of strange poems found by Diamond and his mother on a beach there merely by chance, or is it really a book sent from the country at North Wind's back? Is the evil Old Sal simply Nanny's grandmother or the "salt" in an alchemical process? And, when is a horse not a horse? Well, perhaps when it starts lecturing the horse in the next stall on its greed, or when the other horse turns out to be an angel. Or then again perhaps not: Diamond has just risen from sleep when he hears the horses speak. Yet still, beyond that, we recall that MacDonald thought that dreams and fantasies could be more true to reality than reality itself.

The constant mingling of fantastic elements with the "reality" of Diamond's family life in London begins to make uncertain the final difference between them. This is added to by London itself being made strange, when we find that besides Diamond's family this is a place that has a Mr Dives or a Mr Raymond in it, not to say one that is peopled with alchemical symbolism in the names Mr Coleman, Old Sal, Diamond, and Ruby. Even a lazy cab horse maintains that it is an angel in disguise. This is a world that for all its apparent Victorian solidity is also based in ancient signatures of the mind and the imagination.

Unlike others of MacDonald's fantasies, *At the Back of the North Wind* also gives us different points of view on events. There is Nanny, and also Diamond's mother, who do not believe that his experiences with North Wind were real. There are those who consider Diamond's serene innocence a sign that he is "God's baby" in the sense of being mentally unbalanced. There are others, more pious, who are prepared to believe in Diamond because it suits their faith. There is North Wind, who is resigned to sinking a ship full of innocent people, and Diamond, who is not. And Diamond himself is often uncertain of the truth of his experiences. In no other of his fantasies does MacDonald give so many points of view. They continually show that one view of events is not enough, and leave us unsure of what to believe.

This is also seen in the frequent relativism in the book. When poor homeless Nanny is helped by Diamond and taken to hospital when she is ill, we are inclined to see her as (streetwise) innocence wronged; but she is not only that, for later on she turns against Diamond when she is with her boyfriend Jim, and in her dream she shows herself untrustworthy when she opens a box of bees that cause trouble. In the opposite direction, the cab-man who is a brutal drunkard and a wife-beater comes to see some of the error of his ways, and helps Diamond when he is once in difficulties with cab-men at another station. The Colemans seem good benefactors to Diamond's family, yet they do not provide them with good lodgings, they do not care for children, and Mrs Coleman does not give Nanny a penny at the crossing she sweeps for her. Even Mr Raymond—"Light of the World"—may from one point of view be the rescuer of Diamond's family from misery, but from the human standpoint he is little short of cruel, testing Diamond's father by giving him a bad horse to see how well he survives.

All this relativism can suggest on the one hand that the world is an incoherent moral mixture, or on the other that all human situations added together cannot make any overall sense without reference to God.

At the Back of the North Wind is a very social fantasy. Diamond is rarely on his own for long: the book starts with him meeting North Wind when he is supposed to be alone in bed. No other fantasy of MacDonald's is set in a close neighborhood of people, where everyone and every attitude keeps jostling with others. Indeed, the whole business of cab-driving involves continually meeting strangers. Moreover, no other fantasy of MacDonald's has so much talking in it—to the point where even horses have a conversation. And much of this conversation is in the form of argument and disagreement. Such contrariety can be seen as part of the universe as God's imagination has made it. Equally, it can be seen as expressing a condition of being where nothing is sure.

The book is full of arguments. Indeed, there is no other of MacDonald's works in which people are so keen to stir up or to contradict one another. The story begins with North Wind waking Diamond up and telling him he must follow her downstairs, when there seems no reason why he should. Diamond pesters Nanny with his visions until she herself has a discomposing dream. Meanwhile she herself continually mocks Diamond. The Apostles in the cathedral window stand over the sleeping Diamond and criticize both him and North Wind. Even the horses Diamond and Ruby in their stable have a long squabble about Ruby's supposed sloth and greed. All the characters are forever challenging one other—and this right from the first, when Diamond has let North Wind in through the patched hole next to his bed and then has hidden under the bedclothes:

"I'm not Mr North Wind," said the voice.
"You told me that you were the North Wind," insisted Diamond.
"I did not say *Mister* North Wind," said the voice.
"Well, then, I do; for Mother tells me I ought to be polite."
"Then let me tell you I don't think it at all polite of you to say *Mister* to me."
"Well, I didn't know better. I'm very sorry."
"But you ought to know better."
"I don't know that."
"I do. You can't say it's polite to lie there talking—with your head under the bedclothes."

Diamond himself will not brook prejudice, as when his father mocks his defence of his new friend the drunken cabby next door and his family:

"They're no friends of mine," said his father.
"Well, they're friends of mine," said Diamond.
His father laughed.
"Much good they'll do you!" he said.
"How do you know they won't?" returned Diamond.

At the Back of the North Wind (1870)

"Well, go on," said his father. (174)

At the Back of the North Wind also makes continual use of inversion. North Wind tells Diamond that the hole she makes into his hayloft bedroom is for her a window out from her world into his, whereas Diamond thinks of windows as looking outside to the wide world of North Wind (48). When Diamond and North Wind enter the cathedral on the coast by a door in the tower, this door is so described that it seems they are going out, not in, by it (98). In the story "Little Daylight," the princess sleeps by day and wakes at night. In dreams, Diamond and Nanny see people look in at them from the stars or the moon, but for these people this is looking out, both star-realm and moon being described as spheres. Later we have Diamond reaching the stars by going underground (204–5); he pulls up the "'plumb-line [of] gravitation.'"[19]

Other forms of inversion come from the nature of North Wind herself. The further away from her one moves, the more one feels the cold of her breath; but when one is right up close to her, as Diamond often is, the wind is still, and one can be quite warm. Then there is the odd situation whereby North Wind is least "herself" when she is at home: she becomes weak and helpless, and freezes to a block of ice. For all she is North Wind, she is always going away from the north: she can only get there by shrinking backwards practically to nothing. She flies southwards to find a ship that will take Diamond northwards. And in her very act of blowing southwards she provides sailing ships with the power to travel north. Paradox upon paradox, some found embedded in the nature we know, some in a nature we have not yet seen. All of them turn the world into a perpetual surprise. This is the nature of the universe made by God; and it is also the nature of a universe that continually removes certainty from man. It is also, incidentally, like the fairy tale as Novalis describes it:

> In a true fairy tale everything must be wonderful, mysterious and incoherent, everything bustling and going in different directions[;] ... here is found the time of anarchy, lawlessness, freedom, the natural condition of nature, the time before the world.[20]

MacDonald used these words of Novalis as part of the epigraph to his *Phantastes*.

---

19. MacDonald, *Phantastes and Lilith*, 208.

20. This originates in Novalis, *Die Fragmente* (1805); repr. in Novalis, *Schriften*, III, 454 # 986.

All these inversions and multiple viewpoints may look to a God who ultimately reconciles them; but they also give the impression of a universe that continually upends any attempt to make sense of it, suggesting that any deity behind it could be more cosmic jester than compassionate intermediary.

Just as we have narratives that are continually interrupted, and adventures that are both dreams in bed and journeys abroad, so we find a mixture of stillness and movement throughout the book. North Wind frequently tells Diamond that she has no time to stop and must be about her business, before stopping indeed to have a conversation with him (65–66, 70, 87–88, 96–102). When Diamond is left by North Wind in the cathedral while she goes off to sink a ship, the still figures of the Apostles in the stained glass windows move down from their frames to talk disapprovingly about him; and meanwhile Diamond lies still on the altar steps, at once asleep and conscious and unable to move. At her "home" in the Arctic, North Wind, whose essence lies in movement, is turned into a motionless block of ice. In the inset fairy tale "Little Daylight," the princess dances in the full moon and is torpid and still when the moon wanes. In a poem about Little Boy Blue (176–81), the boy calls together all the creatures and leads them out into the country, only to reveal that he does not know what he wants to do with them, and that they can all go home again: all the movement ends in stasis. Diamond the horse works all he can when pulling a cab, but the other horse, Ruby, is fat and idle. A policeman forever tells people to "move on" who have nowhere to go. Diamond's family moves house in the middle of the story, but then his father becomes bedridden and "still" with illness. Diamond's song about the stream (139–43) flows onwards, and ends where it began, moves forward only to stay. And when Diamond is at the heart of movement with North Wind, he is still. Flying in a nest in her hair in the very core of a storm,

> It seemed to Diamond . . . that they were motionless in this center, and that all the confusion and fighting went on around them. Flash after flash illuminated the fierce chaos, revealing in varied yellow and blue and grey and dusky red the vapourous contention; peal after peal of thunder tore the infinite waste; but it seemed to Diamond that North Wind and he were motionless, all but . . . [her] hair. It was not so. They were sweeping with the speed of the wind itself towards the sea. (96)

At the Back of the North Wind (1870)

The experience is at once physical, an anticipation of human flight, and mystical, partaking in the nature of the unmoved mover.

Stillness and movement also interchange in the way that there both is and is not a story of spiritual growth in the book. Diamond is the perfect innocent from the outset, and yet his innocence is also seen as inadequate, needing refinement. From one point of view, Diamond does not develop, or become "better," throughout the narrative, even if he gains more knowledge, because he is perfect already: he is "God's baby" both when he starts and ends, which is why North Wind comes to him; and his very name, Diamond, suggests the unchanging and pure. When he becomes a cab driver, his simple goodness, humility, and charity still shine through, bringing even the most brutish driver among his fellows to amend his life. And at the end he is still the child nestling to North Wind's bosom and asking to be comforted. And North Wind herself, who has been continually "subversive" in appearance, now tiny, now vast, now omnipotent, now helpless, now a wolf or a tiger and now a loving woman, is still to Diamond the same mixture of teasing girl, beautiful lady, and caring mother that she was when he first met her.

Yet at the same time, there is a contradictory pattern beneath the story suggesting that Diamond is purified, and that there is movement through growth. This pattern comes from alchemy, with which MacDonald was familiar from his reading of Paracelsus and particularly Jacob Boehme.[21] This is one of the deeper narratives of *At the Back of the North Wind*. There are three stages in the narrative that parallel the three of alchemical transformation: nigredo (black), the breakdown of the original substance; albedo (white), or the making of a new substance out of this reduced material; and rubedo (red), the purification of the new substance to the *prima materia*.

---

21. Alchemical symbolism (see Lyndy Abraham, *A Dictionary of Alchemical Imagery*) has a child as one symbol of the stone that is changed; has coal as the fuel of the furnace and as a symbol for the blackness of the *nigredo* (the Colemans, first employers of the family); it sees a house, particularly a glass house, as the alchemical vessel; views wind as an essential part of the reaction; considers bees to be the fiery action by which metals are transformed to the *prima materia* that makes the philosopher's stone; regards trees as symbols for the growth of the stone, and nests as the alchemical vessel it which it is engendered. All these items are prominent in *At the Back of the North Wind*, together with other alchemical symbols such as the moon or Luna, the sun (Mr Raymond, "light of the world"), angels (Ruby the horse, the dragonfly in the well), circles (the princess's dances in "Little Daylight"), sand and sea (Diamond at Sandwich), star (Diamond's dream), stream (the long poem), garden (the Colemans'), serpent (the poem about Little Boy Blue), tower (The Mound), thick and thin (the fat and the lean horses (257–58)).

In *At the Back of the North Wind* these stages are first, Diamond's adventures with North Wind, nearly all by night (black); then his life in London, almost all in daylight (white); and last the ruby ring Nanny is given in hospital by a lady visitor, the ruby glass in her dream and the arrival of horse Ruby (red).[22]

All the contradictions, inversions, arguments, and opposites in the book can suggest a living universe of God, but equally they can convey a living chaos, a continual uncertainty and the absence of coherence. We might know which view we would choose while we are quietly reading this book, but we would probably lose hold of it as soon as we were immersed in the battling currents of the actual world it describes. On one side, the God-centered and "certain" view is that the world is founded on what in the Renaissance would have been called a *concordia discors*. This is epitomized in North Wind, who while often working to destroy things, does so in order to create others. Though she wrecks a ship full of people at sea, she hears the dead becoming singers in the great song that is always coming nearer; and though the ship takes the fortune of Mr Coleman to the bottom, its loss teaches him humility and greater kindness. But this idea of loss countered by spiritual gain still leaves us with the immeasurable nature of grief that knows little consolation in this world, and with a God who works by motives that are often indecipherable to humans. It is the strength of *At the Back of the North Wind* that while it leans to divine answers in which our woe is assuaged, it admits the contrary view of a world in which God seems absent. And there is no "ultimate truth" or higher reality in which these opposites will be reconciled: they lie beside each other to eternity.

Therefore, there are two conflicting conclusions to be made about this book. First we can, and want to, say:—"*At the Back of the North Wind* is unique in its mixture of historical and fantastic realities. The book has 'fantastic' and 'realistic' halves to show that the two are really joined—that our own everyday world is surrounded and interpenetrated by others, and that the distinctions we make to keep reality separate from fantasy are empty. Fiction itself in the form of this story, dreams, poems, inset fairy tales, all are as solid as our 'real' world, all bring us news of another country to which we more truly belong. In a larger view, our world is a dream in God's mind as much as Diamond's experiences with North Wind. In the smaller world of

---

22. For a full account, together with biblical context, see Smith, "Old Wine in New Bottles"; Smith, "MacDonald's Crystal Palace"; and Smith, *The Downstretched Hand*, 17–67.

At the Back of the North Wind (1870)

struggle to which most of the characters are confined, life seems enmeshed in uncertainties and contradictions. And yet out of its impoverished heart, Victorian London produces a child who is God's baby, a new Christ whom those about him fail to understand, a dia-mond or two-world soul, who increasingly moves towards a world beyond ours. Meanwhile, London itself is inhabited by living alchemical symbols, that transform it from a meaningless assemblage of colliding selves to a crucible of slow refinement. Deep within the world the incarnation continues, reminding those who have eyes to see that the ultimate truth of the universe is that heaven and earth are married."

Thus one conclusion. The second, complementary, conclusion might run thus: "This is true, sublimely true of the story, but so at the same time is its opposite. Neither can stand true on its own: the God-based answer is the one most canvassed by the story, but the hard facts of life the story admits, and the contradictory, relativistic, inverted, and fragmentary mode in which it is written, no more suggests a just and loving God beyond our knowledge than it does a world without meaning. No answer is given to the problem of suffering in the world save an approaching song that North Wind only thinks she hears, and a belief that those killed by God's providence are the happier for it afterwards. As much as Diamond may really meet North Wind, she is also a dream begotten of his infancy or his sickness or of his simply being asleep. The fragmentary mode of the story does not express the chaos of a divinely based imagination so much as a world and a mental landscape of which no sense can be made and in which no organizing purpose long survives."

And that is the final paradox of *At the Back of the North Wind*. There is no other of MacDonald's fairy tales in which he so thoroughly discomposes the happy ending that is a traditional part of the genre. All the others are written in a context of the unquestioned reality of the supernatural, but here MacDonald leaves the existence of North Wind and all the consolations she brings ambiguous. Diamond's adventures with North Wind at once take place and are dreamt, and both of those views have to be held together.

In some ways, *At the Back of the North Wind* is a curiously "inconsequential" story. Here is a highly unrepresentative child who, though reared in poverty, speaks "posh," never thinks a bad thought, and remains innocent from first to last; and there, around him, is a society of ordinary, morally mixed humans which in no way influences him. Nor does Diamond change them very much: he is no missionary or Christ figure. By the end of the story he has been elevated to a pet of the bourgeoisie, rather like Dickens's Oliver Twist. His death results in no conversion or transformation of others, it is simply the last step in his withdrawal from the world. Nothing can be made of it in terms of his previous poverty and struggle: it comes out of nowhere as the possible sudden onset of an unstated illness that enables him to die with grace. We cannot make anything of him on this earth, as he is quite unlike most of us, and his adventures quickly make him supernaturally different also.

Yet *At the Back of the North Wind* remains one of MacDonald's most treasured books among readers. And the reason for that is the power of the longing that it awakens in us through Diamond's adventures with North Wind—the longing for peace, for a heaven in which all pains will be understood and laid to rest, the desire for a world that will make sense after all the doubt and uncertainty that beset us: and above all a wish to follow Diamond's spiritual journey, ever growing towards a joyous understanding of earth and heaven, even if half the book denies that this is possible. On this level, the whole of *At the Back of the North Wind* is one long symphony, in which the struggles and doubts of humanity are overwhelmed by the song of an approaching new world in which all sorrows will be assuaged. There is no certainty, no reason in this indiscriminate desire, which denies all the grim side of the text: but it will not be silenced. For it is the desire of all people, whether or not they believe in the reality of its object.

4

The Princess and the Goblin (1872)
The Imagination in the Self

At the Back of the North Wind was set in a dingy Victorian London, *The Princess and the Goblin* looks much more like a traditional fairy tale, with a medieval setting, a royal heroine, a fairy grandmother, evil goblins, and a happy ending. It is more unambiguously mystical than the previous book, without its metaphysical speculations and doubts, and does not involve itself with the topic of death. It is generally felt to be the happiest of MacDonald's fairy tales for children.

Here we find that the imagination, embodied this time in the fairy grandmother the young heroine Irene meets, is again central to the story. But here it is seen among other mental faculties—reason, will, and passion—which ideally work in harmony, but here are at first in discord. This mental battle is the allegory beneath the story.

The Princess and the Goblin is based on the traditional notion of fairy people trying to kidnap women, and also ultimately stems from myths of subterranean beings stealing people of the surface for their own—notably in the stories of Orpheus and Eurydice and Pluto and Proserpina.[1] In MacDonald's story, the goblins live in mines and dig into the house in which young Princess Irene lives, to seize her and make her the wife of their Prince Harelip. This idea is common in Victorian times in the frequent transla-

---

1. There have been two commentaries drawing closer parallels between MacDonald's story and the Persephone myth in the light of the psychology of Jung. For a fuller account, see Appendix B.

tions of such stories of the Grimms as "Snow-White" or "Rumpelstiltskin," and from Dickens's "The Goblins Who Stole a Sexton" in *Pickwick Papers* (1836) to Mrs Juliana Horatia Ewing's "Amelia and the Dwarfs" (1871). Indeed, the year before *The Princess and the Goblin* first appeared in book form saw the publication of Bulwer Lytton's *The Coming Race*, the story of a technologically far advanced people living beneath the earth and planning to take over the world.

The Victorians, it is well known, were continually and fearfully aware of the potential for revolution among the downtrodden proletariat, for whom their numerous charities were in part sops to Cerberus.[2] While MacDonald is rarely political in his writing, in *The Princess and the Goblin* he does tap into a social current of his age. His temperament, while often socialist towards individuals, is more laissez-faire towards groupings of people. In *Robert Falconer* (1868), possibly the nearest thing MacDonald wrote to a social novel, the view of poverty is that it is the workings of God's love on sinners rather than a human outrage demanding social and political change.[3] This is also seen in *At the Back of the North Wind*: the individual must help the wretched, but the righting of all wrongs will take place in the next world, not in this one. The idea of compassion for the suffering poor as individuals is fine, but the notion of them calling for their corporate rights is not so readily admitted. In *The Princess and the Goblin*, the princess becomes friends with a miner-boy, and meets and loves his family, but then she leaves for the court. Only after it is announced in the sequel, *The Princess and Curdie*, that Curdie's parents are of royal blood do the two marry. Both "Princess" books describe the preservation of royalty and the destruction of its opponents. The goblins in the first book are seen less as people with a grievance than as grotesques consumed with destructive ambition; and in the second book those who would displace the king are portrayed as creatures of the pit—to which, in the end, several of them are dispatched.

Thus far politics—politics moralized into good and bad, good being those who go with the grain of reality, bad being those who rebel. In this, MacDonald opposes the central belief of his beloved Blake, who asserted in his *The Marriage of Heaven and Hell* (1793) that "Without contraries is no progression," and that "One Law for the Lion and Ox is Oppression": in Blake's view Christianity had divided reason from energy in man, and

---

2. Houghton, *The Victorian Frame of Mind, 1830–1870*, 246.
3. MacDonald, *Robert Falconer*, vol. 3, 115–21.

made the one good, the other bad. The goblins are the energies in *The Princess and the Goblin,* and their ambitions generate the narrative. Their motive, which for MacDonald is the satanic one of injured merit, would for Blake be the revolution of the oppressed.

However, beneath the official moral simplicities of good and bad often found in the Victorian period, a sense of the truth of Blake's view makes itself indirectly felt. The world was becoming too complex for morality to manage. The new science of psychology was from the 1840s beginning to explore the unconscious side of the mind, where images and promptings operated outside the control of reason or the will.[4] One could label these urges "evil" if one wished, but now they were more an essential than a sinful part of human nature, and could not so readily be suppressed. In the same way, science was now insisting that man had an evolutionary ancestry going all the way back to the apes. In such a world, the "heavenward" impulse could not so readily be divided from the "hellish"; but most people still believed that it could. MacDonald was fascinated by the new areas of discovery, which bore out much of what he had read in Novalis and E. T. A. Hoffmann, and he uses the psychology of dreams in all his fantasies: but he usually filters them through his Christian vision—as, for example, in the last chapter of *Lilith*—dividing the unconscious, or as he calls it, the imagination, into good and bad sides, mystical and potentially monstrous, God-inspired and self-begotten.

Few Victorian writers could consciously acknowledge the challenge of the new psychology to moral values, which remained latent in their works. Exceptions are the Scots writers James Hogg in his *Confessions of a Justified Sinner* (1824) and Robert Louis Stevenson's *Dr Jekyll and Mr Hyde* (1886). Hogg writes about a hypocrite who at first sees himself as forgiven for his murder of his brother because he is one of the elect bound for heaven, and then later blames all his actions on the devil. He thus tries to cut himself off from his conscience and continue to live in polite and "virtuous" society, but his unconscious mind tortures him in the form of a devil he cannot shake off, and eventually kills him. In *Dr Jekyll and Mr Hyde,* the official meaning is that Hyde is a monster created by accident and sustained by

---

4. Ellenberger, *The Discovery of the Unconscious,* 202ff., shows how Romantic theories of the unconscious tended to be idealistic, with the unconscious being seen as working in harmony with nature to perfect the individual; but with Schopenhauer, whose influence was not felt till the 1850s, the unconscious is seen as a blind irrational force founded on the primal instinct of sex (208–9). MacDonald evidently starts from the first, while also uneasily admitting the second.

reckless habit; but the less obvious one is that Hyde *is* Jekyll—that he is the repressed and thereby uglified side of Jekyll the respectable Victorian doctor. Here Jekyll tries in vain to separate himself from his own creature, just as many Victorians tried to suppress or hypocritically conceal their own desires. And so their goblin side—Hyde himself is called a goblin—continually emerges in the grotesquerie, caricature, and fantasy of the period.[5] For all his passion for goodness, MacDonald himself, though never a hypocrite, is part of this predicament; for all his commitment to the light, he senses the presence of a shadow from which nothing can relieve him. And in the same way, Princess Irene and the goblins are bound together in a way that the final extinction of the latter cannot deny.

For each is part of one mind—the yearning spirit and the passionate self, each differently imbued with desire. In *The Princess and the Goblin*, the goblins have been banished from the world of men: what is this but to say that men have called certain of their desires evil and thrust them out of sight? So they become misshapen, vengeful, ambitious, and are called evil. Yet the latent other meaning will out.[6] At first, the official moral narrative may seem reflected in the divided nature of the book, the way each goes on in separate chapters without evident relation to the other. For half of the book the concern is with the growing relationship between Irene and her "grandmother," without much reference to the goblins. The other half involves the young miner Curdie and his attempts to find out what the goblins are plotting. It is only really at the end of the story that many of the characters from these separate parts come together, when the goblins invade the house and are repulsed. But the visits to the two areas of the story continually change place with one another: sections with Curdie and the goblins alternate continually with sections on Irene and her grandmother. Here the effect is of an interweaving of the two, and the suggestion is that they are somehow bound up with each other.

Because of their wish for moral absolutes, it was natural that Victorian writers for children should find the fairy tale, with its total distinctions of good from bad, an attractive medium in which to write. And yet it is strange how often fairy stories in the Victorian period have two or more items in their title, which is rarely one word, as if terms were being set in apposition: "Uncle David's Nonsensical Story of Giants and Fairies," *The Hope*

---

5. See Manlove, *Scottish Fantasy Literature*, passim.

6. I owe much of my interpretation here to Tony Tanner, "Mountains and Depths: An Approach to Nineteenth-Century Dualism."

The Princess and the Goblin (1872)

of the Katzekopfs, The King of the Golden River, Granny's Wonderful Chair, The Rose and the Ring, The Water-Babies, Alice in Wonderland, Mopsa the Fairy, Tinykin's Transformations, Speaking Likenesses, and so on down to *Five Children and It, Rewards and Fairies,* or *Peter Pan and Wendy.* So also we have *At the Back of the North Wind, The Princess and the Goblin, The Princess and Curdie*—or even the dual title of MacDonald's 1875 *The Wise Woman: A Parable,* first serialized and later published as *A Double Story.* Compare these with the single-word titles of the adult fantasies *Phantastes, The Portent, Lilith.* Of course, children are more persuaded to read if a title is fuller, for then they have a teasing notion of the contents; but nevertheless, the habitually appositional mode does stand out.

It would appear that in *The Princess and the Goblin* MacDonald was reacting in particular to Mrs J. H. Ewing's "Amelia and the Dwarfs," which had just appeared in *Aunt Judy's Magazine* (1870–71). In this tale, naughty Amelia is haled underground by a number of dwarfs and taught to clear and wash up after herself, to stop breaking things, and to cease being pert. But then she becomes so good and useful that the dwarfs will not let her go, and one of them wants to marry her; only a magic charm saves her and returns her to her home. MacDonald writes a story that inverts this: his princess is the innocent object of a wicked goblin plot. He will use "Amelia and the Dwarfs" again as a more direct template in *The Wise Woman* (1875).

MacDonald does not call his book *The Princess and the Goblins,* as one might expect (and actually many people think), but rather *The Princess and the Goblin.* Since Prince Harelip, the projected goblin husband for the princess, plays no prominent part in the story, this seems a little odd: there is no other goblin that has any potential relation with her. We are made more aware of the princess's use as a bargaining chip for their whole race, which would seem to make the plural title *The Princess and the Goblins* more apt. But, by making it singular, MacDonald at once sharpens the opposition to one between "princess" and "goblin" qualities, while at the same time also suggesting—just as with the two terms in the title of the next book *The Princess and Curdie*—that they are somehow to be linked.

There are one or two other pointers here. Just as the goblins are enclosed in their mines, avoiding the light, so Irene is kept within the house, protected from dark. (The situation recurs in some of MacDonald's shorter fairy-tales, such as "Little Daylight" and "Photogen and Nycteris," where these opposites are brought together.) The goblins have a king and queen, just as do the humans. We notice that the goblin king had a first (human) wife who died giving birth to Prince Harelip; and the human king's wife died sometime after bearing Irene. Both kings have had a similar experience, and both children have been without their mothers—rather as MacDonald himself was as a child. Harelip has possibly been made vicious by his bullying stepmother. In this case, his relation to Irene would not be far different from that of the oafish Hareton to young Cathy in *Wuthering Heights* (1847); and the relation of the two kings might be faintly analogous to that of Heathcliff and Linton—Heathcliff of the dark wilderness and Linton of polite society. We recall too that her father the king sends Irene away to the country just as Linton does when he gives Cathy to the care of Heathcliff. (Possibly even the two Irenes are analogous to the two Cathys, each "grandmother" in relation to the other.)

Then again, we may ask why Irene has been sent where she has no other children to play with (recalling that MacDonald himself never sent any of his children away from their family). Yet, in another sense, there are children all around Irene: for the goblins are in size as children compared to adult humans; they are indeed the lost children of the story.[7] (Perhaps they are even a figure for rude lower-class children with whom a little lady is not allowed to play.) But Irene is sometimes not so unlike the goblins herself. The stairs by which she first climbs to grandmother's attic rooms are "so steep that she went on like a four-legged creature on her hands and feet"[8] (51)—like one of the goblins' creatures. And here we may recall that MacDonald was wont to call his own daughter Irene, for whom this book was written, "goblin."[9]

There are parallels also between the goblins and grandmother, who are the two sides of the unconscious imagination, about which MacDonald wrote in his essay on faculty psychology, "The Imagination: Its Functions and Its Culture" (1867). Both live in the midst of labyrinths. The goblins have a network of tunnels in which Curdie is easily and dangerously lost; grandmother lives at the top of a little stair which is only really to be found when one has lost oneself in the upper levels of the house. Grandmother weaves her thread as the goblins weave their plots. Grandmother's workroom (55) is as bare of furniture as the equivalent one of the goblins (88): each seems as temporary as the other in their habitations.

---

7. Raeper, *George MacDonald*, 329, likens them to "misshapen overgrown children."

8. MacDonald, *The Princess and the Goblin and Other Fairy Tales*, eds. Shelley King and John B. Pierce, 51. References are to this edition.

9. Raeper, *George MacDonald*, 326.

The Princess and the Goblin (1872)

Just as Irene and her grandmother come together across the distances of the house, so the goblins seek to close the gap between themselves and Irene by tunnelling towards her. The story sees this as projected rapine, but it is also the bringing together of opposites, which the "human" side fastidiously abhors. The goblins effectively try to engineer a marriage of divided races—or, in other terms, mental faculties—which is refused. Of course, put like this, it sounds untrue, because the goblins' motives are selfish, their actions involve violent capture, and they themselves, symbolized in Harelip, are hideous and unnatural. But if we recall that it is their division from the rest of human nature that has distorted them, we may be inclined to look beyond the merely censorious reading. In a sense, it is like entropy, the postulated collapse inwards of the universe under its own gravitational pressure; and it ends in an explosion leading to departure from the house.

We might add here that *The Princess and the Goblin* is involved with the dimension of space. The idea of closing distance, abolishing space, pervades the book. Irene grows steadily closer to her grandmother, and the goblins tunnel ever closer to the house. Irene is given a thread by her grandmother that is joined to the dark part of the mine where Curdie is trapped. Much too is said about "room." Caught in the goblin caves, Curdie has little room to turn round; and the same is true of Irene as she follows her grandmother's magic thread into a crack in the mountainside to find Curdie where he is trapped. The goblins are associated with confinement, compression, claustrophobia, weight. The goblin plot ends in their being stifled by material in the form of water. Grandmother, on the other hand, can make the walls of her room vanish and reveal the vastness of space; or can put Irene in a bath that has no bottom but opens on a blue gulf of stars. Everything with the goblins comes inwards and is of earth; everything with grandmother expands outwards and is of air. Yet the two are as necessary to one another as both the expansive and the contractive forces of the universe.

The impression of secret unity among the different characters is added to by the oft-remarked symbolism of the house in which the princess lives and its surroundings.[10] The goblins live mostly underground in tunnels and caves. The princess lives on the ground floor of the house, but ventures four storeys up to make friends with a strange old lady who lives in the attics

---

10. Chesterton, "Introduction" to Greville MacDonald, *George MacDonald and His Wife*, 10–11; Wolff, *The Golden Key*, 166; Prickett, *Victorian Fantasy*, 185; Raeper, *George MacDonald*, 328; Robb, *George MacDonald*, 118.

and says she is her great-great-grandmother, and has come to the house unseen to take care of her. There is a tradition of houses as symbols of the mind going back to Spenser's House of Alma in *The Faerie Queen*, Book IV (1593), and frequently seen in the nineteenth century, in works such as Poe's *Fall of the House of Usher* (1839), Tennyson's *The Palace of Art* (1842), Dickens's *Bleak House* (1853), William Morris's "Lindenborg Pool" (1856), and MacDonald's own poem "The Haunted House" (1883). The landscape of *The Princess and the Goblin* can be seen as symbolizing three areas of the mind, first the good imagination or the soul, then reason and the senses in the middle, and last the "bad" side of the imagination, where twisted ideas and corrupt desires hold sway in the forms of the goblins and their misshapen creatures that emerge as nightmares after dark.

Alternatively, some have put this in non-moral terms, as Freudian *superego*, ego, and subconscious *id*.[11] It is typical of MacDonald that this is not unambiguously so: though the goblins are subterranean, they are not always "beneath" Princess Irene or even her "grandmother," for their tunnels extend up the mountain beyond the location of the house; and the hero Curdie and his fellow-miners also work half their lives underground next to the goblins. Since Princess Irene is at the center of the story, and is the only one to enter all three of these regions, we may say that hers is the human mind being symbolized here, and that this mind contains the goblins no less than the "grandmother" part. The reference of the "mental" imagery of the story to Irene is heightened by the way she is isolated in this story, sent away from her parents and the court (for no convincing reason) to this lonely house, where she is kept in, and where there are no companions of her own age. However, for MacDonald, the larger mind behind the narrative is that of God, whose imagination continually makes the world.[12]

If we follow this mental imagery, what then is happening? After Irene has met her "grandmother" the goblins try to frighten her. Her heart may be brave, which is why she persuades her Nurse Lootie to take her for a walk further up the hill than they should go. But then they are menaced by the goblins. We have a choice here. We can say that Irene is not so afraid as Lootie, who becomes hysterical, and that the two of them are eventually

11. Tanner, "Mountains and Depths," 52–54; Reis, *George MacDonald's Fiction*, 81–82; Prickett, *Romanticism and Religion*, 185–86.

12. "As the thoughts move in the mind of man, so move the worlds of men and women in the mind of God, and make no confusion there, for there they had their birth, the offspring of his imagination. Man is but a thought of God" (MacDonald, "The Imagination," *A Dish of Orts*, 4).

rescued by a little miner boy who has no fear of the goblins and who knows how to drive them off. That is, we can read this simply as the account of three different characters and their reactions to a threat. Alternatively, we can say that the goblins are grotesques suddenly rising from the dark of Irene's unconscious, that Lootie is Irene's own fear, and Curdie her eventual reason and common sense; and that the last overcomes the others. Almost certainly while reading we chose the former, because the characters seem so vivid as individuals, and it is hard, say, to identify the silly Lootie with any part of Irene: but the suggestion of the latter reading is also present, and more present when we look back at the story. One of the graces of this tale is the way we can slip between one level of reading and another without any sense of transition.

In the same way, we can see Irene's meeting with the old lady of the attics as her first encounter with her own "higher" imagination, the imagination that MacDonald often described as inhabited in its furthest recesses by God.[13] In exploring further and further upwards in the house Irene has lost herself, which means she has lost her *self*, the being that thrusts its way between man and the truth. Later she says, "'I went upstairs, and I lost myself, and if I hadn't found the beautiful lady, I should never have found myself'"(61). By climbing to the attics she has found her truer self, a lady whose name is also Irene. She has climbed upwards into her "higher" imagination.[14] If we have read others of MacDonald's works we will know how stairways fascinated him as symbols of ascent towards the spirit. A deep spiritual journey is being suggested through the everyday image of a bored child exploring some stairs and finding an old relative at the top of them.

The young princess has four meetings with her "grandmother," on each of which details quietly change. On the first, dirty from climbing the stairs, she has her face washed with water from "a little silver basin" (55); next time her feet are washed in "a large silver basin" (104); on the third encounter she is shown "a large oval tub of silver" (119), and on the fourth

---

13. MacDonald, "The Imagination," *A Dish of Orts*, 1–5, 18–19, 24–25.

14. In his biography of MacDonald, his son Greville recalls a conversation on symbolism in which his father said that a symbol was not an arbitrary sign of a conception, but shared a common substance with what it represented: "So may we find co-substance between the stairs of a cathedral-spire and our own 'secret stair' to the wider vision" (Greville MacDonald, *George MacDonald and His Wife*, 481–82). Stairs are also symbolic in this way in "The Golden Key" and *The Princess and Curdie*: one ascends into one's own spirit.

she is immersed in it and washed all over (156). It is a progressive baptism, in which she sinks deeper and deeper into the holy imagination. And alongside these changes, more and more of the lady's nature is revealed. At first, she seems to Irene a very odd relative living on her own, living on pigeons' eggs and spinning. But then, when the princess next meets her, grandmother says she did not find her again till now because "'I didn't want you to find me'" (99); she speaks of the thread she spins with as coming from spiders "'of a particular kind'" from far across the sea; she shows Irene her unexpectedly magnificent bedroom; and she says that the moon by whose light she works is to most people invisible. From being strange or odd in the first interview, grandmother has become rather wonderful.[15]

In their third meeting, this wonder is turned to supernatural awe. Irene finds the old lady now transformed to a beautiful, young, golden-haired woman, dressed no longer in black but rich blue, with a fire whose flames are shaped like roses, and whose bedchamber has walls that dissolve; she gives Irene a ball of invisible thread she has been spinning, telling her always to follow where it leads her. Their last encounter occurs after Irene has taken Curdie the miner to meet her grandmother and, angry at not seeing her, he has left. This time the atmosphere changes from the supernatural to the holy. Now grandmother gives Irene a mystic experience beyond anything she has known before, when she lays her in her bath with no apparent bottom to it:

> When she opened her eyes, she saw nothing but a strange lovely blue over and beneath and all about her. The lady and the beautiful room had vanished from her sight, and she seemed utterly alone. But instead of being afraid, she felt more than happy—perfectly blissful. And from somewhere came the voice of the lady, singing a strange sweet song, of which she could distinguish every word; but of the sense she had only a feeling—no understanding. Nor could she remember a single line after it was gone. It vanished, like the poetry in a dream, as fast as it came. In after years, however, she would sometimes fancy that snatches of melody suddenly rising in her brain, must be little phrases and fragments of the air of that song; and the very fancy would make her happier, and abler to do her duty. (156)

15. The transformation from old woman to beautiful lady seen here is also seen in Curdie's experience of her in *The Princess and Curdie* as he grows in spirit; and in the changing view of the harsh-seeming old magic lady in *The Wise Woman* as Rosamond improves. The idea ultimately derives from the folk tale motif of marrying a hag who turns to a beauty.

The Princess and the Goblin (1872)

This is Irene's form of the experience little Diamond had at the back of the North Wind, and the song he heard in the stream. It is an intuition of heaven, symbolized in the blue color all about her. Throughout Irene has been journeying deeper into her own imagination, portrayed in the changing aspects of the lady and her surroundings. Finally giving herself up to it, as she does when she yields herself to being placed in the bath, she approaches the edge of something great at the center of her mind and the world alike.

This, however, is only one side of the symbolic narrative. On the other is Irene's relation to the goblins, who represent the darker side of her imagination. Here it will seem harder for the reader to accept what the imagery implies, because Irene is so much made the innocent child and the friend of her mystic grandmother, and only once encounters the goblins. But here it is not Irene herself but Irene in her "higher" imagination that has met the grandmother. This is why Irene's every meeting with the mystic lady is prefaced either by the possibility that she is dreaming, or by the presence of another with her who cannot see the lady while she does. What she sees is what her imagination sees, but what the imagination sees is, for this story, more real than sight. There are other parts of Irene's mind—the goblins, Lootie, Curdie—that the story itself means us to think of as separate people when they are not merely that. One problem for the story is precisely that Irene's various faculties are so separated: and in the end they all come together, though more in a collision than as a unity.

The goblins, who were once driven underground, are the side of mind that cannot be admitted in the lives of pure Victorian maidens. Indeed, during the story Irene is, in her imaginative self, to banish the goblins further. For, following the invisible thread her grandmother has given her, she overcomes her fear of them, enters their dark and labyrinthine world, and rescues Curdie, who has penetrated their realm and been trapped by them. For most of the narrative Irene's reason and commonsense in the shape of Curdie have tried to keep this dangerous imagination "under," and to frustrate it by working out where it may erupt. But in fact these efforts are in vain, for only the higher imagination can foresee and circumvent the actions of the lower. So it is also that when later the goblins break into the house, it is grandmother, not Curdie, who thwarts them and removes Irene to a safe place. They are then thrust back to the depths by the operation of Curdie as reason, which has found out their weak spot. In the end, this dark side of Irene's mind is entirely removed, through the destruction of the goblins in the flood.

The modern reader will protest at this: how can the dark unconscious mind be treated as an outsider, how can it be destroyed when it is an essential part of the mind? But we forget that for all his interest in the unconscious, MacDonald did not see things this way. For him, this area of mind was associated with evil and worldly desire: it was only what he saw as the "higher" unconscious, the one that here goes upstairs rather than down, that is to be explored. His psychology operated through a Christian prism. We think of our desires as part of what we are: he thought of them as something to be controlled or turned to good. MacDonald would here have rejected the views of Freud and Jung. It all depends on one's notion of the self: MacDonald thought of the self, considered as a separate entity, as a chimera; one only gained one's true self by giving it to God. To us, in their quest to seize the princess, the goblins can even be felt to be Promethean in their daring; or, in another view, a side of the mind that has been made ugly trying to recover beauty. While at one level the story opposes such readings, on another it admits them.

All this still leaves Curdie, who so far has been seen as "reason"—which in no way makes him any less a human boy, honest in character, brave, commonsensical, downright, and amusing. Also, unlike the goblins, he is an agent of rationality in that he mines ore for the benefit of the kingdom: the goblins by contrast dig and sell nothing, and, apart from their nefarious plots, would probably do nothing. Most of all Curdie is an empiricist, who believes only in what he sees. His common sense and his senses alike tell him that Irene's great-great grandmother does not exist, when according to Irene she is right in front of him in her attic workroom. He is the part of Irene that always demands proof and sensible evidence, and has no truck with the imagination and with faith. As such, he has to go back downstairs where he belongs. But Irene's reason and empiricism must themselves be converted before she has complete faith, and thus the companion-book, in which Curdie is transformed, will be part of Irene's transformation too.

Indeed, one of Curdie's problems in *The Princess and the Goblin* is that he is left to operate on his own, and by his own lights, which are as a candle in the dark of the mine. MacDonald wrote in "The Imagination" that "the Intellect must labour, workman-like, under the direction of the architect, Imagination," and "It is the imagination that suggests in what direction to make the new inquiry."[16] The physical string, the string of sense, by which Curdie would find his way out of the darkness of the goblin tunnels, is displaced by the goblins' creatures in their play, and he is lost. That is, Irene's reason, finding no direction, gives way to fancy, and loses its thread, leaving it at the mercy of chance. Chance, in its ambiguous way, then does two things: it puts Curdie, as all his searches could not, where he can at last hear something of the goblins' secret plot; but it also brings about an accident by which he is captured and imprisoned in a hole by the goblins and cannot do anything about it. There he remains until Irene reaches him, and her thread of imaginative faith shows that there is in fact a gap in his prison by which he could have escaped. In other terms, Irene's imagination finds a way where reason and her senses could not.

But then the other faculties are closed in on themselves compared to the "higher" imagination, which always opens out. The dark mine tunnels lit only fitfully by candles symbolize this. The goblins have shut themselves away from men. Curdie, though he detests the goblins, is familiar with them, and for half his days shares their kind of existence. As Blake says in *The Marriage of Heaven and Hell*, "everything would appear . . . as it is, infinite," but for man having "closed himself up, till he sees things thro' narrow chinks of his cavern." As we have seen, by contrast, the spiritual imagination continually expands: grandmother's nature grows ever larger as Irene gets to know her.

Curdie is as noble as man's natural faculties are noble, but no more, and his mind operates only along one track. He does, at the end of the story, however, begin to use that area of the imagination that MacDonald considered to be behind the construction of any scientific hypothesis.[17] Till then he has learnt the second goblin plot (to flood the human part of the mines) by overhearing it, but has never discovered the first, which is to capture Irene. However, he now puts separate facts he has learned together to conclude at the goblins may be tunnelling towards the house. He tries to test this by listening at night to try to hear beneath in what directions the goblins are digging: but on the very night that he becomes certain that his guess was correct, he is shot in the leg by one of the king's archers, who mistakes him for one of the goblins' creatures. Now helpless, even his warnings are useless, for the guards do not fully understand him and think he is raving from his wound. (Thus, Curdie is disbelieved just as

---

16. MacDonald, "The Imagination," *A Dish of Orts*, 11.
17. MacDonald, "The Imagination," *A Dish of Orts*, 12–15.

he disbelieved Irene before.) Once again, his lack of true imagination, his myopic concentration on one thing to the exclusion of all others, leaves him vulnerable, here literally. Meanwhile, the goblins successfully dig their way into the house, only to find their own ignorance: for being unaware of the grandmother's presence, they expected to find Irene in her bed. The divine imagination that comprehends everything cannot be understood by them.

As seen, in Freudian terms the goblins are part of the mind of Princess Irene: yet they are rejected and destroyed in this story. In this sense, at the end of the story, though Irene's "higher" imagination has been transformed by her meetings with the lady of the attics, she is lacking in this other area of the spirit. In Blake's terms, "Those who restrain desire, do so because theirs is weak enough to be restrained; and the restrainer or reason usurps its place and governs the unwilling. / And being restrained, it by degrees becomes passive, till it is only the shadow of desire."[18] Officially, the story denies this and the princess is its unambiguous heroine; unofficially, Blake's dialectic works within it like a suppressed desire. The result we see in *The Princess and Curdie* is that Irene lacks character, except as the devoted daughter, and Curdie first meets her again when he can hardly recognize her in the shadowy bedroom of her father. She has become Blake's "shadow of desire," her love for her father more to her than anything else. She and Curdie never speak of their own love for one another, and all we hear at the end is that "Irene and Curdie married" (219), and then that "they had no children," which is not surprising. In addition, during that story, lacking the common sense and imaginative insight of Curdie, Irene has been taken in, more even than her sick father himself, by the false masks of his evil counsellors, and has been ignorantly allowing them to poison him.

It is actually Curdie who becomes the more complete hero in *The Princess and Curdie*. We have here a better instance of the "Intellect labour[ing] workman-like, under the direction of the architect, Imagination"[19] in the way that Irene's grandmother takes the increasingly cynical and materialistic Curdie in hand, transforming him into an acolyte of the imagination. And in this story the darker side of the imagination is not rejected but tamed, and works as part of a divine creation. The hideous and vicious dog Lina and the monsters and grotesques who leave their dark wood to join Curdie on his way to Gwyntystorm are the goblins transmuted to

---

18. Blake, *The Marriage of Heaven and Hell* (1793), sect. iii.

19. MacDonald, "The Imagination," *A Dish of Orts*, 11.

benevolent use. At the same time, they are the nightmares produced by sin. For here the enemies are not within the self, but without, in society.

In parallel with its separation of faculties, *The Princess and the Goblin* has separated areas of action. The princess in the house or with her nurse Lootie, the princess with grandmother in the attics, Curdie in the mines, the goblins in their caves or digging their secret tunnel, Curdie's parents in their house, all these places only occasionally meet, as with Curdie's incursions to the goblin mines, Curdie's failed visit to the attics, or Irene's rescue of Curdie from the mines. Curdie's doings have nothing to do with Irene till late on, and Irene's activities with her grandmother go on without knowledge of Curdie. Irene is sent to rescue Curdie at just the time he has begun to guess that the goblins' main scheme is aimed at her. They have as it were been tunnelling in their own directions, and finally these tunnels have intersected.

All the characters, apart from the lady of the attics who overlooks and manages them all, are in ironic situations, ignorant of the workings of others. For long Curdie does not know the goblin plot to capture Irene, Irene knows nothing of Curdie's activities in the mine, Curdie cannot believe that grandmother is present in the attics, the goblins are not aware that Curdie has discovered their scheme to flood the mines if their first plot fails. At the same time, these plots are isolated in the story in the sense that they have no final influence on its outcome. Curdie's hard-won discovery of the goblins' threat to Irene cannot be communicated, because he has been wounded and put out of action at the critical moment. All the goblins' plans to capture Irene fail, because grandmother knows what they are about and removes the princess. And the goblin plot to flood the human mines is overheard by Curdie, who has the place where the water will break through so blocked that the water fills up the goblins' mine and drowns them. It may be added that the goblins' entire tunnelling scheme seems as orotund as their discourse, for there was little to have stopped them overrunning the house by night from above ground, even with the added guards.

The fact that actions are so often futile or circumvented lends a certain stasis to the book. By contrast, in *The Princess and Curdie* all Curdie's efforts to save the king from being poisoned by his counsellors are successful, and there is only one core action going on, not a series of them. The ultimate reason for all this is that *The Princess and the Goblin* is about being, not becoming. The condition of existence in *The Princess and Curdie* is change, whereby Curdie is changed from being a materialist to a believer in the invisible truths of the world, and all creatures and men in the book are seen as continually able to alter their inner natures by their actions. In *The Princess and the Goblin*, however, the medium is not so plastic in this way. Legend has it that the goblins' long residence underground has made them more grotesque than when they lived on the surface, but the narrator declares, "The goblins themselves were not so far from the human." And any physical change there is comes from their damp dark environment rather than from any moral choice made by them (48–49). During the story itself, apart from grandmother, who changes from old to young woman through Irene's visits to her, no one else alters aspect in the slightest. They are as they appear, and that is all.

And when grandmother changes in appearance before Irene in the story, it is not that she is "becoming" something different, but that she is revealing more of what she is. And in the same way, young Irene is not so much changing as realizing her potential.[20] *The Princess and the Goblin* is a gradual revelation of the true natures of things. Through several meetings grandmother, as it were, dilates from a quaint relative to a lady of supernatural and ultimately Christian power. In Curdie the strengths and weaknesses of the natural man of reason and common sense are explored. The goblins, seen at first as partly comic, show their innate viciousness as they try to enact their schemes. And through contact with the lady of the attics, and through her behavior, Irene is able to discover the true princess that is in herself. The book is rather like an early seventeenth-century masque where individual characters reveal the living ideas that work through them.

At the same time, the book is full of questions about what is seen. It continually interrogates "being." Who is the strange old woman in the attics? How did she get there, how does she live, what does she do, where does she sleep, where does she get her silk for spinning? How did the goblins get into the mines? Why are they so ugly? Why are their creatures so grotesque? What are their plans? The goblins have peculiarities, such as their detestation of poetry, or their orotundity, or their sensitive feet and rock-hard heads. The meetings between Irene and her great-great-grandmother are as idiosyncratically human as they are symbolic. Always we are looking at the extraordinary nature of things as they are. When grandmother tells Irene that she eats the eggs of her white doves, the princess replies,

---

20. Contrast Lesley Willis Smith, *The Downstretched Hand*, 136: "She [Irene] becomes not simply an older Irene, a more powerful Irene or an Irene who has changed direction, but a new creation."

"Is that what makes your hair so white?"
"No, my dear. It's old age. I am very old."
"I thought so. Are you fifty?"
"Yes—more than that."
"Are you a hundred?" (58)

But the main question about reality in the book of course concerns whether or not grandmother is "really" there. Irene has to learn to believe that she is real and not a dream even when she is away from her, and Curdie cannot believe that she is real even when she is right before him. The same goes for Irene's thread, which leads her in and out of the mines by ways Curdie himself could not have found, and which he himself cannot feel. Lootie, who thinks that Irene is making up stories about a lady in the attics, is a constant source of distress to Irene. Curdie's mother tells him that she has cause to believe that grandmother is real, and that he should not judge Irene when he cannot himself be certain of the limits of the world. We even have an almost parodic version of believing in the reality of what cannot be seen in the goblin queen, who, having kept her human feet invisible in shoes, demands that the goblins believe that her feet are as lacking in toes as theirs. But the goblin queen is denying reality with a lie, where grandmother is enlarging reality with a higher truth.

The official object in the book is to keep things as they are. It is deeply conservative. Grandmother, who has come "'to take care of [Irene],'" protects her from the goblins so that she may remain princess in the upper world and not become one in the lower. Irene continues the royal line and the past, which her great-great-grandmother, also called Irene, exists partly to symbolize. The goblins must be thrust back to the place where they belong. Any insurrection must be stopped, including Nurse Lootie's attempt to gain authority over Irene (165–66). In the end, even Curdie will not accept the promotion to court offered him, but chooses to remain with his parents.

At the close, as in some comedy, the plots and characters come at last together, and all is revealed. The goblins and their underground world come to the house, Curdie is there too, the king arrives, and Irene is safe in Curdie's parents' house. All the aspects of Irene's nature, wanted or unwanted, are together in one place. Now we stand outside the house, which is still a symbol of Irene's mind, and see it invaded by the flood released by the goblins. It is Irene's final symbolic immersion in water: her whole being is cleansed and purged, her spirit and royal person are now complete. That is what the story asks us to believe. But as the bodies of the slain goblin race wash out of the doors and windows we see her failure in the midst of her success. The dark side of her mind has not been understood, nor reconciled with the rest of her being, it has simply been expunged, in a kind of frontal lobotomy of the spirit. The book ends with a sense not of unity but of dissolution, as Irene and her father leave, and Curdie wrongly refuses the king's offer of a job at court. Now we have entered the world outside the "centripetal" house that has fixed all interest till now, the world where people are no longer aspects of Princess Irene, but separate individuals with lives of their own. This more fragmented and lonely world of free will and choice is the darker spiritual context of *The Princess and Curdie*.

5

The Wise Woman (1875)
The Imagination against the Self

First serialized under the title "A Double Story" in *Good Things: A Picturesque Magazine for Boys and Girls* from December 1874 to July 1875, MacDonald's next fairy book was quickly brought out in 1875 by Alexander Strahan, the publisher of all his previous children's books, under the title *The Wise Woman: A Parable*. This is more a long short story than a full-length book; only large type spread it over the 222 pages of the first edition. Though this story has not been so popular as others of MacDonald's children's fantasies, it has a hidden beauty and wisdom, like the wise woman herself, who is grim and rough only on the surface; it was included by C. S. Lewis among MacDonald's "great works."[1]

The Wise Woman is in the idiom of the two "Princess" books that appeared before and after it, being set in an imaginary medieval kingdom in which two girls, one royal, one a shepherd's daughter, both badly behaved, are taken by a strange old woman to her magic cottage in the wilderness where they are tested and punished to try to reform them. This woman is like the old grandmother in the other "Princess" books, in that she is similarly mysterious and of supernatural power. Here though, she goes about hidden in an old cloak and seems much more harsh. This is partly because the children she is going to deal with have gone far more wrong than Irene or Curdie.

---

1. Lewis, ed., *George MacDonald: An Anthology*, Preface, 17.

George MacDonald's Children's Fantasies and the Divine Imagination

Coming after the innocence of Diamond in *At the Back of the North Wind* and the cheerful view of children in *The Princess and the Goblin, The Wise Woman*'s picture of two wickedly selfish girls seems strange. Even when set in the "real" world, MacDonald's work never directed itself at evil children—witness *Alec Forbes of Howglen* (1865), *Guild Court* (1868), *Robert Falconer* (1868), *Ranald Bannerman's Boyhood* (1871), or *Sir Gibbie* (1879). It is possible that MacDonald was underlining his distinction between the child and the childlike;[2] possible that, working at home as he did, he was becoming irritated by his own eleven progeny, ranging from under ten to teenage; possible too that he was suffering long-term exhaustion from his often harrowing lecture-trip to America in 1872–73. Added to that was his struggle with illness through the winter of 1873–74, and the sudden serious fever of his daughter Mary in 1875. On the other hand, the years 1873–74 are remembered by Greville MacDonald as "among the happiest spent at The Retreat" (the family home by the Thames at Hammersmith).[3] And it should be noted that the darker idiom of *The Wise Woman* is continued in the very pessimistic view of humanity in *The Princess and Curdie* (serialized in 1877), and even beyond to the picture of human evil in *Lilith* (1895).

MacDonald's 1867 essay on the imagination is called "The Imagination: Its Functions and Its Culture." MacDonald has dealt with the nature and *functions* of the imagination in his shorter fairy tales and in *At the Back of the North Wind* and *The Princess and the Goblin,* showing its different areas and levels and portraying its workings in the world and the minds of more or less innocent child characters. In *The Wise Woman*, he turns to the *culture* of the imagination. This involves learnt behavior, the central concern of *The Wise Woman*. "Nothing will do so much for the intellect or the imagination as *being good*."[4] The whole of *The Wise Woman* is a training in being good, leading to the growth of a good imagination. It is not an easy course for its subjects, and only one of the children at last stumbles into a pass grade.

Because this story is taken up with the highly resistant evils of its child characters, it has little of the mysticism of *At the Back of the North Wind* or *The Princess and the Goblin.* Where they deployed the "good" imagination

---

2. MacDonald, "The Child in the Midst," *Unspoken Sermons*, 2–6. In "The Fantastic Imagination" MacDonald declares, "I do not write for children, but for the childlike, whether of five, or fifty, or seventy-five" (317).

3. Greville MacDonald, *George MacDonald and His Wife*, 465.

4 MacDonald, "The Imagination," *A Dish of Orts*, 36.

in the form of beautiful women with sublime powers, here the wise woman is a seeming old crone until one of the girls, Rosamond, begins to reform: at which she is seen as a beautiful and ageless lady. Throughout the story the wise woman has been disguised because she is among people who cannot see good—rather like Edgar in *King Lear*. She is the true beauty of the imagination that both children have been without.

The moral drive of the book against the bad behavior of two pampered children has seemed excessive to some commentators, who find a tone of harsh moralizing in the story that makes it unbalanced. The impression is even that MacDonald is indulging in a vengeful attack on bad behavior with a fairy woman who abducts and tortures two recalcitrant children to try to reform them. Here, it is felt, MacDonald has lost his temper, and proceeded to an elaborate moral indictment quite disproportionate to the facts.[5]

However, in the wider context of nineteenth-century children's literature, the story is not the exception it looks. In the modest amount of (usually morally analytic) criticism so far written on *The Wise Woman*,[6] it has not so far been observed that it belongs to a tradition of nineteenth-century children's conduct fantasies—and it is by no means as censorious or punitive as some of them. These stories were designed to educate their readers in good behavior in the world by showing naughtiness punished by figures drawn from the imagination—fairies, goblins, giants, and sometimes monstrous versions of the self. The energies of the fantastic imagination were used to heighten evil and more strikingly convey its consequences.

Simply being good like Irene in the other "Princess" books, or the innocent Diamond in *At the Back of the North Wind*, or Prince Dolor in Dinah Mulock's *The Little Lame Prince and His Travelling Cloak* (1874) was often not enough: one had to be seen to become good and to do good to others. Perhaps the earliest Victorian example is Elizabeth Sinclair's "Uncle David's Nonsensical Story of Giants and Fairies" in her *Holiday House* (1839), where the idle boy No-book is delivered by the Fairy Do-nothing to the Giant Snap'em-up, to be hung by his hair in the giant's larder prior to

---

5. Particularly Wolff, *The Golden Key*, 168–70; see also Reis, *George MacDonald's Fiction*, 84–85; Zaitchik, Preface to George MacDonald, *The Wise Woman* (1977), vi; Carpenter, *Secret Gardens*, 83.

6. See Anon., "The Wise Woman as an Agent of Identity in George MacDonald's Story *The Wise Woman*"; Battin, "Duality beyond Time"; Holm, "Tendering Greatness: George MacDonald's *The Lost Princess* and the Bible"; Jarrar, "*The Wise Woman, or The Lost Princess*." For a summary of these writers' views, see Appendix C.

being consumed, until the sight of the Fairy Teach-all and her happy little charges on a sunny hillock outside changes his ways. The child does not develop in any natural manner, but is hammered into shape by the fantasy. However, here the comic grotesque flavors and sometimes partly obscures the moral.

This impulse to improve the child reader, often by sending the characters to fantastic reformatories, is continued through such books as the Reverend Francis E. Paget's *The Hope of the Katzekopfs: or, The Sorrows of Selfishness* (1844), the translation of Heinrich Hoffman's *Struwwelpeter* (1848), Margaret Gatty's *The Fairy Godmothers* (1851), Kingsley's *The Water-Babies* (1863), Annie and E. Keary's *Little Wanderlin and Other Tales* (1865), and A.L.O.E.'s [A Lady of England's] *Fairy Know-a-bit: or, A Nutshell of Knowledge* (1866). Mrs J. H. Ewing's moral tales "The Land of Lost Toys" (1869), "Amelia and the Dwarfs" (1870), and "Benjy in Beastland," appeared in her *The Brownies and Other Stories* in 1871. They are respectively about the correction of children who will not care for their possessions, treat animals kindly, or clear up after themselves. They are aimed rather more at instilling good manners than morals; but nevertheless they are a strong influence on the form and method MacDonald uses in *The Wise Woman*. Indeed, the account in "Amelia and the Dwarfs" of a little girl being dragged away from home by goblins to learn by force the housework she will not do at home was almost certainly adapted by MacDonald.

All of these stories set the imagination against the evils of their child characters in order to reform them. And they are usually shown to succeed, with grotesque images and experiences that terrify the fictional child into conformity. Near to MacDonald in time is the story in Christina Rossetti's *Speaking Likenesses* (1874), where spoilt little Flora's birthday party becomes quarrelsome and violent, and she, escaping it, comes upon another and more fantastic birthday party where all the children are covered with quills, fish-hooks, or sticky or slimy fluids. These horrors express the feelings displayed at Flora's party. The frequent punishments of bad children in Victorian fantasy could become excessive or even sadistic: no doubt the reason for this was that such stories dealt with the stubborn everyday naughtiness of children, and the authors had painful experience of the gap between too stringent rules and often intractable reality.

However, even if the grotesque form of the imagination is used to reform children—greedy infants being eaten by giants, naughty children turned into dandelions, ever-lengthening noses, slate pencils, carrots or sponges, disobedient children driven from their home by the replacement of their mother by a monstrous one with a huge wooden tail[7]—all this still leaves the imagination as the enemy, for it pictures the moral distortions of children, their distance from good behavior, through a world turned upside down. Good behavior involves conformity, modesty, and restraint, all representing the subjection of the individual to a collective, and all equating virtue with good sense rather than the life of the imagination. In this way, Victorian Evangelical hostility to the imagination is continued, even while that faculty is used to heighten a moral lesson. But MacDonald's *The Wise Woman*, while it uses the imagination to picture evil, also shows that the good life is ultimately founded on the divine imagination rather than merely on obedience to societal precepts.

The story to which MacDonald seems particularly indebted is Francis Paget's *The Hope of the Katzekopfs*. Paget's story describes a pampered prince called Eigenwillig (Self-will), only son of King Katzekopf and the aptly named Queen Ninnilinda, whose behavior grows so gross that he even insults his fairy godmother Abracadabra. She removes him from his parents and his royal home, determined to reform him, just as happens to Princess Rosamond in *The Wise Woman*. After a range of physical tortures, including Eigenwillig's being pulled into a string through a royal keyhole and then rolled up and kicked about as a football, Fairy Abracadabra leaves him in Fairy Land to the tender mercies of the parasitic dwarf Selbst (Self) and the increasingly attractive ideas of an old man called Discipline.

In *The Hope of the Katzekopfs*, the lessons are made explicit by the figure of Discipline, who utters them in bold Gothic print: "'Learn to live hardly; Deny yourself in things lawful; Love not comforts; Think of others first, and yourself last.'"[8] But *The Wise Woman* has no such easy morals. The two heroines have very individual forms of evil which require quite different methods to defeat; and every moral decision is difficult in a way that renders mere obedience to a mnemonic irrelevant. Mere habit itself that thickens evil, is hard to overcome; injured merit, that thinks itself ill-treated beside another, will brook no humility; self-complacency, shown its own evil, will only bend like seaweed in the tide.

---

7. Respectively, Sinclair, "Uncle David's Nonsensical Story of Giants and Fairies" (1839), Annie and E. Keary, *Little Wanderlin and Other Stories* (1865) and Lucy Lane Clifford, "The New Mother," *Anyhow Stories* (1882).

8. Paget, *The Hope of the Katzekopfs*, 204.

MacDonald is much truer to the moral complexities of real life, and offers no easy or self-pleasing answers. In his story, he has not just one but two very different characters, whose self-love shows itself in quite different ways: and both are very stubborn. Despite some backsliding, Paget's Eigenwillig quickly reforms, improving in more or less a straight line; but in *The Wise Woman*, Rosamond's victory over herself is only a beginning, and Agnes becomes, if anything, worse. The two girls are continually slumping back into their old selves; and the story itself mirrors this process, going back and forward from place to place, from palace to cottage to palace, and to and from cottage and shepherd life. MacDonald is no simple moralist: he knows well how the human soul works, and his analysis of the constant slippage of Rosamond's small improvements is acute. Particularly effective is his emphasis on doing good whatever one's mood.[9] His portrait of Agnes's continued evil despite her own knowledge is really frightening and dreadfully accurate. For all the weight of the fantastic devices brought to bear on her, she remains what she is. It is not the least of the story's power that it retains so stubborn a sense of human reality in the most fantastic of situations.

In *The Hope of the Katzekopfs*, Fairy Abracadabra, Selbst, and Discipline are moral trainers with a clear program: input one refractory boy prince into a moral production line and arrive at a man who is king over himself. Indeed, there is a sense that Eigenwillig's new self is made by others rather than himself. But in *The Wise Woman*, the lady may take the children away from their corrupting parents, and may show them what they are truly like: but she cannot change them herself, she can only lend a hand when they have chosen the right way for themselves. The whole object of the fantastic devices in his story is to reveal, not to perform.

However, simpler in approach though *The Hope of the Katzekopfs* may be, Paget is one of the few children's writers to direct his attack at the root cause of evil, love of self; and this is also MacDonald's theme in *The Wise Woman*. Like the self-willed prince who meets himself in the repulsive dwarf Selbst, each of MacDonald's heroines has been brought up to think herself Somebody, and each is led to meet that self and see just how repellent it is. But again, MacDonald's characters see more of the complexities of the situation: as Rosamond puts it, "'I hate myself, and yet I can't help being myself!'"(292).

---

9. MacDonald, *The Complete Fairy Tales*, ed. Knoepflmacher, 292. References are to this edition.

The Wise Woman (1875)

Like Paget, who uses fantastic images of Eigenwillig being helplessly pulled through a keyhole or used as a football to show how little importance his vaunted self really has, MacDonald gives us a cottage full of strange trials that his young protagonists Rosamond and Agnes undergo and mostly fail. These include a sphere containing nothingness, into which Agnes is placed for three days, a gallery of pictured locations that the observer can enter at will, and a series of "mood chambers" where Rosamond's powers of self control are tested in various scenes in which she is an actor. The image becomes part of the moral, giving it a force it might not otherwise possess. But the difference with MacDonald's story is that such images are more than mere fictional devices, they picture a supernatural reality. The wizened child that Agnes meets in the featureless sphere in which the wise woman puts her for three days is her soul, which she has shut away all her life.

At first it might not seem that this story has much to do with the imagination inside us. The wise woman does not appear to be part of either girl's mind. She does not seem to be conscience, for both girls have no conscience, although Rosamond develops one. She is described as coming many miles from her home to the royal palace or to the shepherd's cottage, and appears more of a force of correction from outside. Yet this old woman, who seems so remote from the two girls, is in fact from the depths of their own minds in which, however bad they are, God has his dwelling. She has travelled up from this dark region into their conscious, "at home" selves to care for them when they cannot or will not care for themselves, and cannot see what their souls most desire. The more she seems separate from them, the closer she is to them. MacDonald says,

> In the gulf of our unknown being God works behind our consciousness. With his holy influence, with his own presence, the one thing for which most earnestly we cry, he may be approaching our consciousness from behind, coming forward through regions of our darkness into our light, long before we begin to be aware that he is answering our request—has answered it, and is visiting his child.[10]

However, the story is also concerned with the workings of the divine in the world outside the self, the world made by God's imagination. There is a strange passage at the beginning of the book that images the wise woman's nature. The narrator is describing rain falling. In a certain country, "in the midst of a shower of rain that might well be called golden" a princess is

---

10. MacDonald, *Unspoken Sermons*, 255–56.

born. The reference is most directly to the myth of Danaë, whom Zeus seduced in a shower of gold; but for some Renaissance iconographers that in itself could be a pagan figure of the unceasing grace of God.[11] In *The Wise Woman*, however, this rain falls not only as a golden shower, but elsewhere in the bleaker mountain parts of the country "the same cloud that was dropping down golden rain all about the queen's new baby was dashing huge fierce handfuls of hail upon the hills"; and beneath this, another baby is born to a shepherd's wife. These two forms of rain symbolize the two forms of grace descending—on the one hand, as a comforter to afflicted good, and on the other, as a shock to the sinner. It is pleasure for those who try to obey God and Christ, pain for those who do not. It is also, at the level of geography, purely obeying natural law in the different ways it falls, gently on the rich country, harshly on the poorer part: no pathetic fallacies here. Its two aspects are contained in the mysterious wise woman, who makes evil painful and good the soul's delight: she is divine grace working within nature and the mind to bring men and women back to their true source.

The wider context of the story, in which the old woman comes from the wilderness to court or country, is as we have seen also the image of a journey from the depths of the imagination. The mental reference of the story is much more immediate when we come to her cottage. Princess Rosamond ("Rose of the World"), who broke away from the old woman during her journey, finds when she arrives at the cottage that she cannot get in because it has no door. At length, it occurs to her—she who has never had to ask for help before—to knock with a stone on the wall: and as soon as she does so she finds herself striking a door that opens. The biblical reference seems plain: "to him that knocketh shall be opened" (Matt 7:8; Luke 11:10). Rosamond has entered her own imagination, which is also God's imagination working in her.

And she is made to learn that while her hostess is absent she must keep the cottage clean, stoke the fire, and regularly water her heather bed to keep it fresh. The reference here, so immediately physical in terms of housework and food as reward, is also a picture of how Rosamond, in cleaning her inside house out will also nourish her soul. (This process is none the less true for the fact that it does not work with Agnes, whose housework only increases her complacency: Rosamond has to struggle against herself

---

11. For example, Abraham Fraunce, *Amintas Dale* (1592), 14: "Danae may represent man's soule, and Jupiter's golden showre, the celestiall grace and influence deriued into our mindes from aboue."

to do the work, whereas for Agnes, who is used to it at her own home, it presents no difficulty.) At first Rosamond fails, and but for the old lady's magic fir-cone keeping the fire alight, she would have been torn to pieces by the creatures of the air she hears raving round the house all night.[12] These creatures are the darker forces of the imagination, which seek to take over the better part and come closer the more neglected it is: "If the dark portion of our own being were the origin of our imaginations, we might well fear the apparition of such monsters as would be generated in the sickness of a decay which could never feel—only declare—a slow return towards primeval chaos." "But," MacDonald continues,"The Maker is our Light."[13]

In this story, MacDonald has given a particularly clear picture of the divinely based imagination. Behind a large old clock in the cottage Rosamond sees a door; and squeezing behind the clock is able to get out (she goes into a region beyond time here). But she has not gone outside, but further in:

> Instead of the open heath, she found herself on the marble floor of a large and stately room, lighted only from above. Its walls were strengthened by pilasters, and in every space between was a large picture from cornice to floor. She did not know what to make of it. Surely she had run all round the cottage, and certainly had seen nothing of this size near it! She forgot that she had also run round what she took for a hay-mow, a peat-stack, and several other things which looked of no consequence in the moonlight. (251)

And we are told that "Had the princess been tolerably tractable she would by this time have known a good deal about the wise woman's beautiful house, whereas she had never till now got farther than the porch. Neither was she at all in its innermost places now." Here we have an image of the divinely based imagination, growing larger while going further and further in.

In one of the pictures in the hall Rosamond sees a pastoral hillside scene, with a shepherd and his dogs, sheep and lambs feeding, and a little girl playing in a brook. Entranced, she resolves to go there, and after looking at the picture a long while no longer believes it to be a picture but a reality, into which she steps over the frame. She finds herself outside the cottage, with the door gone, and the sheep-covered hill before her. She has,

---

12. This fire recalls the fire that preserves the mid-sea cottage in *Phantastes* when it sinks beneath the waves (ch.xix).

13. MacDonald, "The Imagination," *A Dish of Orts*, 25.

in going through the picture, apparently gone through the imagination to reality. But at a deeper level she has gone into a reality that was pictured.[14] And here the world is revealed as a work of imagination also. And, we are left to ask, whose imagination is that?

Later, the shepherd's girl Agnes (from "agnus," a lamb) repeats this process, and chooses to go through a picture showing Rosamond's royal home. However, unlike Rosamond, she takes no notice of the extraordinary hall, only of the images and what they can offer her: she sees she can do well for herself at the palace. She has no sense of wonder, that first condition of imaginative awareness, only of want, whereas Rosamond wanted to go to the pastoral scene because it delighted her. Both girls desire their scenes, but Agnes's desire is of quite a different nature from Rosamond's. When Agnes goes through the picture "a terrible storm of thunder and lightning, wind and rain, came on. The uproar was appalling" (266).

The motif of insides and outsides, of being inside a room or a house or outside in the wide world, is one that runs through the book. Inside the construct of the house there is a measure of control and order: fires are to be made up, hearths swept, furniture and floors dusted, beds made up, and mattresses sprinkled. Outside, in the world of wild nature and uncontrolled mind, wolves and unknown monsters lurk in the dark. If the inside of the house is left uncared for and disordered, if the soul is neglected, the dark forces outside come closer and seek to enter: only the ever-burning and hidden hot fir-cone in the fireplace stops them from coming in by the chimney. That fir-cone is God's presence in the deepest part of the soul.

Yet there are also wild things within the cottage itself in the shape of human passions and vanities that are far darker even than the things outside. The violent tempers of Rosamond whenever her will is thwarted, and still more the quiet, well-mannered wicked complacency of Agnes, are far less easily banished than wolves. The rages of the king and queen in their palace, and the fatuities of the shepherd and his wife in their cottage are alike images of the morally dangerous self.

Perhaps the most striking image of the dangers of the inner world is in the revelation of herself given to Agnes. Rosamond has no true self, only a series of ungoverned impulses: she is uniquely sensitive to what the

14. C. S. Lewis probably took this idea from MacDonald in his *The Voyage of the "Dawn Treader,"* ch. 1, where the children walk into a picture of a galleon at sea that turns out to be real. The whole idea of a gallery of pictures entering any of which takes one to a different world was also used by Lewis in his *The Magician's Nephew*, ch. 3, where there is a wood full of pools, immersion in any of which brings one to a different universe.

world outside her gives or withholds, and acts like a slave to her moods. The problem with Agnes, however, is that she is all self. Her evil lies in what she *is* rather than what she is not; it lies within, and does not show itself in acts. She is not subject to discipline from outside; the only way she may be changed is simply by showing her what she horribly is. That is why on bringing her to the cottage the wise woman wastes no time but immediately places her in the spherical chamber that is the inner world of her soul. There is nothing in the sphere, not even a solid floor: nothingness characterizes being in here. Gradually all sense of place, of time, and of direction is lost, and Agnes is totally isolated from the world. All she has is her mind, of which the sphere is a symbol, and her sense of herself as "Somebody." The more she considers herself Somebody, the more she makes herself Nobody: the nothingness in the sphere is her own. And after three days Nothing itself takes form and sits down beside her.

Agnes has now met her true and stunted spiritual self, a naked child with her chin on her chest; she is "the colour of pale earth, with a pinched nose, a mere slit in her face for a mouth" (63), and it makes Agnes shudder.[15] When Alice says anything, the creature emptily repeats it,[16] and Agnes realizes this is herself. Each time she attacks the child it vanishes, to return ten times more hideous than before. Agnes has to sit with this self for another three days, seeing all her sin in the other's behavior, until she is let out. Through this image we see how the innermost heart of a person can be far more demonic than the most terrible horror from outside—and more powerful, because it lives at the heart of the inside from whence to work out, like a worm in an apple (254, 265).

Agnes is, in one sense, like the children of other Victorian fairy tales who are confronted with themselves—the idle children of "Uncle David's Nonsensical Story," Tom the sweet-stealer shown covered with prickles in *The Water-Babies*, Benjy punished by the creatures he tormented in "Benjy in Beastland." But where these reform entirely, Agnes does not. Horrified by her vision of her self, she may be "ashamed of the life she had hitherto led . . . and astonished that she had never seen the truth concerning herself before" (261), yet she remains as she is. MacDonald has a deeper view of evil: the imagination may be awakened to terror, while leaving the evil will intact.

---

15. J. K. Rowling will use this child as the remnants of Voldemort's soul at the end of *Harry Potter and the Deathly Hallows*, 2007.

16. Like the Un-man in C. S. Lewis's *Perelandra*, 140–41.

There is a parallel trial for Rosamond later in the story. The wise woman takes her beyond the big hall to a circular room with many doors, through one of which she pushes her, telling her that she is in a mood chamber. What Rosamond has to learn is how to go against her own arrogance, hasty temper, and possessiveness—in short, she must learn to command herself. But the difference is plain: she must change her behavior, where Agnes must change her perception. By now the small motions of the spirit she has begun to show in the story qualify her for the tests. A sign of this is that the wise woman, who for most of the story has been away from Rosamond, is now actively present in her training.

During her trials in the mood chambers, Rosamond fails when she tries to manage on her own. In the first chamber, she is back in her palace home and when her nurse tells her that she cannot see her parents she loses her temper and hurls a pet rabbit at her, whereupon the nurse reveals herself as the wise woman. In the next chamber, she is boating on a lake with a little boy when a violent squabble develops and she throws him overboard, accidentally killing him in the process. His grieving mother eventually reveals herself as the wise woman. However, before her third trial Rosamond asks the wise woman to help her, and this time she succeeds. MacDonald said, "It is the upstretched that meets the downstretched hand,"[17] referring to the Christian notion that will of itself is not enough without divine grace. This time Rosamond is with a wonderful child in a garden, and growing angry at her own insufficiency is about to fall into a rage and do harm, when a whisk from the child's pet horse knocks her over and gives her time to reflect on what she is doing and repent. She makes friends with the child, who turns into a beautiful form of the wise woman.

In all three of the mood chambers, nature or animals are present—the pet rabbit Rosamond throws in the first, a garden landscape with flowers and a lake in the second, and in the third "a forest, a place half-wild, half-tended," with the wondrous child and the winged horse. We notice how the natural world increases through these chambers, from a pet rabbit in a room to a forest that is so natural that it becomes supernatural. These shifts perhaps symbolize Rosamond's becoming steadily more open to the possibility of overcoming her self. While earlier she withered the flowers about her with her desire to pick and possess them, now, when she touches a silvery flower in innocent pleasure at its life, it grows, opens, and turns gold. Reality becomes fantastic, and nature mingles with supernature. For

---

17. MacDonald, "A Sketch of Individual Development," *A Dish of Orts*, 72.

MacDonald, the natural world, the creation of God, is full of grace, and mirrors the imagination in which God is at the root of things. To love and where appropriate submit to nature is to go out of the old self into a new one where mystic relations become possible. MacDonald said that "every fact in nature is a revelation of God";[18] and of the unacknowledged gifts that nature daily gives us, "One day, I trust, we shall be able to enter into their secrets from within them—by natural contact between our heart and theirs."[19] Yet there are those such as Agnes the shepherd's daughter who, surrounded by nature all their lives, long only for their self-advancement in the town.

We can see how *The Wise Woman* is not simply a story of the attempted correction of two children, but a vision of good and evil in the mind and in God's creation. The book moves between the extremes of the infernal vision of herself given to Agnes, and the image of restored paradise Rosamond is finally able to see in the last mood chamber; and it shows that "There is no word to represent that which is not God, no word for the *where* without God in it; for it is not, could not be."[20] In its moral and spiritual complexity, and its picture of divine grace all about us if we will open our hearts, *The Wise Woman* is one of MacDonald's most profound and yet lucid creations.

One aspect of the subtlety of the book is the way that evil is seen as a function of the faculty that begets goodness—the imagination. Both Rosamond and Agnes believe that they are "Somebody"—that is, they live by that aspect of the imagination called "delusion." We saw this at work in the short fairy tale "Cross Purposes" in chapter 2, above, only there we called it "illusion," because it involved someone tricking someone else. Delusion really involves deceiving oneself; and it becomes evil when the self-deception involves a grandiose or complacent view of what one is. This is the truth about Rosamond and Agnes: both think themselves "Somebody," Rosamond arrogantly, Agnes complacently. So too their parents, with their belief in the wonder of their children, which is a way of making themselves wonderful through their children. This is the selfish imagination, the imagination of the pit: and it must be changed to the imagination that lies outside selfishness, the imagination that can see how small it is, and how great the created world about it—the diverse world of lowlands and uplands, city and

---

18 MacDonald, *Unspoken Sermons*, 463.
19. MacDonald, *Unspoken Sermons*, 351.
20. MacDonald, *Unspoken Sermons*, 611.

country, rain and shine, and grace everywhere. So this story is about the imagination taking arms against the evil side of itself.

The Wise Woman was from the first called *A Double Story*. Most evidently this refers to there being two contrastive heroines of high and low position who have been brought up differently. Rosamond and Agnes are seen not only by themselves, but have homes and parents in the world, though they ignore or defy them. We start with them in these homes, a palace and a cottage; each visits the other's place during the story; and at the end they are returned to their own homes to live out their lives. The ultimate concern of the book is the purification of their souls and their imaginations, but there is also emphasis on their relations with others and with the world in which they live. Rosamond is the spoilt child she has been partly through being indulged by her parents, who will be blinded by the wise woman. The pride Agnes's parents have taken in her has transferred itself to her as spiritual complacency. Rosamond is to serve her parents, helping them towards better insight, while Agnes's mother is to be punished by further seeing how evil they have made her. The story has to deal with the outer world as well as with the inner one, for the aim is to make the two girls better able to live well in it. MacDonald has cleverly reduced the potential duality between the inner and outer worlds, the world of the spirit and the world of everyday life, by having the girls go to the palace and the countryside directly through pictures in the gallery behind the cottage clock. In other words, they enter the "outside" worlds as pictures created by the imagination.

The two contexts might also have been divided by the fact that in the wise woman's cottage Rosamond's and Agnes's evils are addressed in terms of their personal responsibility for them, whereas in the court and with the shepherds the girls' parents are treated as the sources of their wickedness. But what seems opposed is not really: the children have been made the way they are, but they have also chosen the easy ways of egotism. This is one of the double visions of the book. (In this part-blame of the parents, *The Wise Woman* stands out among Victorian children's stories, which nearly always blame the child.) Similarly, in her cottage the wise woman controls the children and they are the authors of their own fates. In the divine world truth is never "either/or" but "both/and." That is what doubles are ultimately for in MacDonald's work, to show how divine truth includes and transcends them both.

The Wise Woman (1875)

The theme of the imagination in *The Wise Woman* is also seen in its movement from illusion to revelation. The story begins with the illusion of one's importance or singularity to which people are prone. First, it establishes the idiom of reality in this book:

> There was a certain country where things used to go rather oddly. For instance, you could never tell whether it was going to rain or hail, or whether or not the milk was going to turn sour. It was impossible to say whether the next baby would be a boy, or a girl, or even, after he was a week old, whether he would wake sweet-tempered or cross.

The natural response to these supposed oddities is that they are not peculiar at all. That one should be unable to predict the future is the condition of our and, so far as we know, any world. So the statement that this world is peculiar by being ordinary confounds itself. It is an odd opening for a children's story, but it is implying that nothing and everything under the sun in God's universe is special.

In an appropriately pompous and orotund manner, the story continues: "In strict accordance with the peculiar nature of this country of uncertainties, it came to pass one day, that in the midst of a shower of rain that might well be called golden...." More than a page follows of one huge suspended sentence that wanders about describing the quality of the rain, the plants and flowers it falls on, the washing it does of the air, and its reception by flowers, stones, sheep, and even a hedgehog; until at last,

> While the rain was thus falling, and the leaves, and the flowers, and the sheep, and the cattle, and the hedgehog, were all busily receiving the golden rain, something happened. It was not a great battle, nor an earthquake, nor a coronation, but something more important than all those put together. *A baby-girl was born;* and her father was a king; and her mother was a queen; and her uncles and aunts were princes and princesses; and her first cousins were dukes and duchesses; and not one of her second-cousins was less than a marquis or a marchioness, or of their third cousins less than an earl or countess: and below a countess they did not care to count. So the little girl was Somebody.... (226)

The description, which might well have been the prelude to the arrival of a god, or even of Christ himself, falls on its rhetorical face with this conclusion: all these other happenings with the rain end in a mere "something happened." Again, the idea that the event was somehow peculiar or special decreases any significance the princess's birth might have had; and anything important in her very existence is diminished to vanishing point with the shrinking levels of rank of those more distantly connected to the throne.

With this, the whole idea of a world or an event that is more singular or important than another is by now denied. And in the process, by the description of the rain falling, we have been reminded of how the world is a living harmony in which the rain gives life and health to all things equally, from flowers to hedgehogs. (Though it is interesting that no mention is made of the various people it falls on.) This idea of free giving sets a spiritual yardstick for a story that will be about selfishness.

Now we move to a very different sort of rain, and an upland country with much less luxuriant vegetation. This rain is hard and cold, driven by strong winds and often takes the form of hail which it dashes in "huge fierce handfuls" on the hills. Here everything cowers from it or takes shelter. But still it does good, if here to a bleaker and treeless world of prickly furze, broom and heather; and it comes from the very same cloud that we saw distributing such richness upon the lowlands. The analogy with God, who instructs through both pleasure and pain, is evident. And we are soon going to meet the incarnation of this dual nature in the wise woman.

In this countryside, which is described in a similarly suspended sentence to that which approached the birth of Princess Rosamond, another child is born, this time to a shepherd and his wife, and she too is regarded as Somebody. The very use of the vague word "Somebody" conveys emptiness: the child may be wonderful, but until it learns humility it will in fact be nobody. This baby "had not an uncle or an aunt that was less than a shepherd or dairymaid, not a cousin that was less than a farm-labourer, not a second cousin that was less than a grocer, and they did not count further" (227). This, of course, points back to the absurd value put on rank by Rosamond's family, and also shows that vanity is not the sole possession of royalty. Everyone has delusions of their own grandeur. The value put on connections by people contrasts with the connections made by the rain, which falls equally on all people.

The human world portrayed in *The Wise Woman* is obsessed by wants. Instead of being happy with what they have, people want more. The description of nature that begins the book shows all the gifts of life that are freely given and sustain us: and yet nobody, save the animals and the vegetation, notices them. But people are driven by what is not present: by delusions about their own importance, the wonder of their children, by ambition, greed, envy, and even spite. They lose touch with common realities. Princess Rosamond wants the moon, which is an impossibility, so her parents make for her a large thin disk of polished silver which they tell her is the moon. But when one day she sees through the illusion, Rosamond is furious, unable to accept that she cannot possess the reality. We are told too that when her wish for something is satisfied, she soon tires of it. It is the mental life of longing for an object that gives it a spurious radiance that disappears as soon as it is realized. Here the imagination, used in the service of the self, can be an evil.

And yet it is also true that Rosamond is in a spiritually more open position because her life is based on desire for she knows not what. Her unsatisfied longings tell us that her desire goes ultimately beyond the things of the world, though she is far from knowing this. She at least wants the moon; Agnes considers only herself, and is satisfied, like a contented lizard on its belly (255).

During the opening passages of the book the narrator punctures his (or her—it could equally be the wise woman herself speaking) own illusions. Instead of giving us a straight description, he keeps thrusting himself upon our notice. An elaborate description of the raindrops being turned as they fall to molten topazes, and a ramble into the various golden-colored flowers that each drop might make, is followed by a dragging back to the central topic in "while this splendid rain was falling, I say . . . ." But then the narrator diverges again to natural description in a whimsical account of horse chestnuts, sycamores and flowers, talks of the effect of the rain in washing the air clean of smells and disease, and describes the different sounds rain makes—until, abruptly, he checks himself with the realization that he is here stealing ideas from someone else, namely Coleridge: after which he returns to his description, which is by now clearly not just a description but a constructed artifice of which he has broken the illusion. He is watching himself construct a scene and laughing at it and himself. A little later, when painting a picture of how the harsher rain in the hills falls on "dry prickly furze and its flowers of red gold, or moister, softer broom with its flowers of yellow gold, and great sweeps of purple heather, mixed with bilberries and crowberries and cranberries," the narrator suddenly stops: "—no, I am all wrong: there was nothing out yet but a few furze-blossoms, the rest were all waiting behind their doors till they were called . . ." (226–27). Again the illusion is broken, and again we are made aware of the author who has been constructing it.

This illusion-breaking narrator is present throughout the story, entering it to tell us what is really going on, or to provide moral interpretations of events. The king and queen are apparently distracted when Rosamond disappears from the palace; but we learn that the hearts of people in that country are so strangely fashioned that if the voice of the princess was heard in one of the corridors, their first reaction "would have been a jump of terror" (231). The story is suspended while we speculate on alternative events. Later, when Agnes is being taken away from her home wrapped in the wise woman's cloak, she is not frightened, thinking that she will soon be set down and is too important to be injured: at which the narrator inserts a paragraph discussing whether it is a good or a bad thing not to be afraid, and describing how "The fearlessness of Agnes was only ignorance" (258). We may regard this as intrusion, and consider that it would have been better if it had been dramatized within the story rather than made explicit. But intrusion, the breaking of the self-enclosed nature of story, is the point here. If we say that this is just MacDonald intervening morally, as he does in others of his stories, it must be replied that in this story it is done for a particular purpose. The islanded self, whether a narrative or an arrogant child, must be broken down and integrated with others. That is why the story deals with a rich city girl and a poor country one. It is also why we have the elaborate natural descriptions at the outset of the book, for they show how all things in nature grow in harmony and in rain or shine.

The wise woman is in one way truth, even while she works through the imagination. Her clothing beneath her cloak is that of Una in Spenser's *The Faerie Queene* (I, xii, 22), "All lilly white, withouten spot or pride, / That seemd like silke and silver woven neare; / But neither silke nor silver therein did appeare" (*The Wise Woman*, 229). Here the clothing represents purity and humility; but Una herself in Spenser's poem mainly stands for truth, which dispels the delusions of the imagination to which Redcrosse, the hero of the first book, is particularly subject. By drawing attention to Spenser's first book here, MacDonald is underscoring the preoccupation of his own story with delusions of the imagination that must be dispelled by truth.

However, like Spenser, MacDonald attacks only delusion concerning the self, not the illusions created by the imagination to serve a larger spiritual purpose. Of this the primary example is the story itself as a fiction designed to transform both the characters inside it and the reader outside. The wise woman herself uses illusion in order to reform her charges. When

The Wise Woman (1875)

the recalcitrant Rosamond is left alone outside the cottage and finds that it has no door, she has to knock as though it had a door to gain admittance. The cottage itself is full of picture-making devices. Agnes is put into "a great hollow sphere," made of a substance "no one could see by itself. It had neither door, nor window, nor any opening to break its perfect roundness" (259). We have seen how this is an image of her soul, which she must enter to find out what inhabits it. In its perfection it may also be a picture of heaven, in whose light the true nature of the diseased soul is exposed. But most immediately it is an illusion, one that is the only way of exposing reality. And like some mid-Victorian photograph, the image of her soul takes a long time to appear. Actually, the sphere is described as being made of the same substance as the mirror that showed Rosamond her true inner self until she smashed it (248). The mirror, unlike the camera, shows the object before it immediately: this may be saying that Rosamond's evil is as immediately present as her rages, where Agnes's evil lurks hidden from her much further within. Whatever the case, illusions and images are being used to reach otherwise unobtainable realities.

Rosamond and Agnes live by false illusions. They have ideal images of themselves that they project on to the world. This is shown in their behavior in the wise woman's picture gallery beyond the cottage clock. Rosamond is delighted by her self-projected picture of a summer countryside with green hills, streams, sheep and a shepherd, and in the center of it a little girl building a stone bridge across a brook. She longs to go there, presses towards the picture and actually enters it. But what she finds on the other side is no country idyll but a wilderness in which she comes near to starving, and is only rescued when Agnes's mother, looking far afield for her missing child, comes upon Rosamond instead. Later Agnes also enters the wise woman's magic picture gallery, and is herself charmed by a picture—her picture—of the city and the court where Rosamond lived. She, however, finds her hopes of self-advancement there completely dashed.

Towards the end of the story, we find illusions serving another purpose. Having taken the still recalcitrant Rosamond from the shepherd and his wife back to her cottage, the wise woman introduces her to her "mood chambers." As we have seen, the primary purpose of these chambers is to put Rosamond in situations that test her self-control: and by the third she is able to make one small gesture that carries her at last towards the right. But this is not all that is going on. The mood chambers in sequence present a growing picture of potential happiness. The first is of Rosamond's old nursery, with her old nurse by the fireside and her toys on the table; the second is a lake in a garden with a beautiful boy playmate; and the third is a forest full of wonder. But it should be said that the chambers are overlapping: each time Rosamond is pushed through the same door in the circular hall (112, 116). The chambers thus stand in stacked rather than merely alternative relation to one another.

Through the three we travel further away from ordinary experience of the world to reach a realm where, instead of dying, things can be given new life, and where beneath a tree sits a girl with eyes "as full as they could hold of the laughter of the spirit—a laughter which in this world is never heard, only sets the eyes alight with a liquid shining" (289). This girl throws flowers from her lap to take root where they fall; but Rosamond finds that the flowers only die when she touches them. Besides this, there is a winged pony that gives delight to Rosamond; but also jealousy when she sees its preference for the other girl. We are in the land of myth, with the flower goddess Demeter/Ceres and the flying horse Arion, fathered on her by Poseidon/Neptune. But more than this, we are in the realm where the pictures of the imagination become visions of divine truth. In a sense, we have journeyed through the three chambers of the imagination to its deepest level where, as MacDonald believed, God lived. And at the ends of the three visions, the wise woman appears, first as the old royal nurse, then as a grieving mother, and finally, growing up from the fairy child in the vision to "a woman perfectly beautiful, neither old nor young; for hers was the old age of everlasting youth" (125).

In *The Wise Woman* as a whole we travel through deepening pictures of the imagination, from the self-deluded pictures of themselves held by Rosamond and Agnes, to the pictures of their innermost selves given to them by the wise woman, to the vision of the self transformed afforded to Rosamond. The process is one of deepening revelation, with the wise woman as artist creating images to reform and heal the spirit. The evil imaginations of the girls come from the deluded self; the wise woman creates images that reveal the soul's true nature and a world of joyous self-giving that far transcends the self-pleasing visions of her charges. That her much greater imagination has a good chance of changing Rosamond's selfish one, whereas it has as yet little influence on Agnes, is part of the "Double Story" that is real life.

6

The Princess and Curdie (1882)
The Imagination against the World

The Princess and Curdie was first serialized in 1877, two years after the publication of *The Wise Woman*, and continues its moral tone, though more widely and somewhat more harshly. Because Rosamond and Agnes were seen as examples of self-love and bad parenting, the censorship did not go beyond them and their families. But though *The Princess and Curdie* starts with judgment on the individual insensitivities of Curdie, it later becomes an indictment of most of the inhabitants of a whole society. The evil involved here is that of acquisitiveness, whether for gold or a kingdom—a sin more of adults than of children. The impact of both good and evil is now wider and more universal. A princess was under threat in the earlier book; but in *The Princess and Curdie* a whole kingdom is on the point of collapse. Rosamond on her own may be improved, and Curdie also: but when it comes to adults the emphasis in both books is more on punishment than on reform. And since most of *The Princess and Curdie* takes place among adults—even Curdie and Irene are now young adults—the book is darker throughout. It would be fair to say that of all MacDonald's children's books, *The Princess and Curdie* is the least suited to the label. That may be why it has never been quite so popular or so frequently reprinted as *The Princess and the Goblin*.

The Princess and Curdie still retains a good number of the formal constituents of its much more innocent companion story. Most of the main characters are the same—Curdie, the old princess-grandmother, the king, and young Irene. In both books, we start with the big house and its attics, the mines and their environs, and the hillside cottage of Curdie's parents.[1] Just as *The Princess and the Goblin* portrayed Irene's tutelage by the lady of the attics, so Curdie too is educated; and as both of them develop, so does the form of the lady to them, from withered crone to strong young woman. As in *The Princess and the Goblin*, Curdie has adventures in the mines, which alternate with visits to the lady in the attics. Curdie has to find and rescue the helpless king from his enemies in the city of Gwyntystorm, just as Irene in *The Princess and the Goblin* had to search for Curdie in the goblin mines and release him from their trap. Each story also involves mining up into the wine cellars of a house or palace—in the one, by the goblins into the house where Irene lives, and in the other by Curdie digging and scrambling into the cellars of the palace of Gwyntystorm. Both books end with mining that goes wrong and results in a flood that destroys the miners.

In both books too, we find groups of grotesque animals—the cobs' creatures, and then the fifty helpful beasts of *The Princess and Curdie*. Like its companion book, *The Princess and Curdie* portrays the (d)evolution of one species to another; and a part of the human body is a recurrent motif—feet in *The Princess and the Goblin*, hands in *The Princess and Curdie*. But the emphasis on the change from one bodily form to another is more marked in *The Princess and Curdie*. The goblins of the first book only slightly degenerate underground from the shapes they once had, and their creatures are less morally than physically degraded: but in the later book we have people turning into vultures, serpents or foxes, and a grotesque-seeming savage dog, whose inner soul is that of a child.

Central to both books is the action of the divine imagination, personified in Princess Irene's "grandmother'" with her mystic doves, her moon, and her huge and beautiful room whose walls can dissolve. In *The Princess and Curdie*, this imagination is extended to a huge dog and forty-nine fantastic creatures; and it also resides in Curdie's hands, transformed in a mystic fire of roses to act as sensors of evil. As in *The Princess and the Goblin*, there are opposite poles in the narrative—on one side, the imagination; on the other, here, materialism. Between the two—the country house and

---

1. Also, in *The Princess and the Goblin*, we have a secular/sacred contrast between the string that fails to lead Curdie back out of the goblin mines and the mystic thread that leads Irene into the mines to rescue him. Similarly, in *The Princess and Curdie*, the lady of the mines pulls a large stone from the solid rock floor with ease, while Curdie's skill with a mattock is needed to strike away the piece of rock jutting up from the main street of Gwyntystorm.

the city of Gwyntystorm—travels Curdie, who is himself a materialist at the outset of the story before his transformation by the lady. The imagination in this story is more isolated than in *The Princess and the Goblin*: grandmother is seen as an evil old hag by the local miners and their families, and Curdie with his mystic powers and strange creatures is largely on his own in Gwyntystorm.

Despite the narrative similarities, the second book rewrites the first in quite different terms, reversing its largely happy vision. At the start of *The Princess and Curdie*, we do not find the same boyish, reckless Curdie of the first book, nor the Curdie who came to believe in the reality of the old princess: now he is a more cynical, even materialistic teenager, who with his new bow and arrow can shoot a beautiful pigeon while it is resting. People are now coarser—the miners, a rude housekeeper who tries to bar Curdie from Irene's former house, and the folk who stone him as a dirty miner on his way to Gwyntystorm. The "Princess" in *The Princess and the Goblin* is little Irene, but in *The Princess and Curdie* she is rather more the older Irene of the attics. We have moved from innocence to experience. Goblin evil in the first book has no reference to humanity; but in the second we learn about human corruptibility, even that of the good king. Indeed, it is fair to say that in some sense the humans are now the goblins of the first book.

With the emphasis now more on society than on the individual, we find that in the second book we spend much time in a city, where in the first book we were in the country. In *The Princess and the Goblin* the concern is with the interaction of different characters, where in *The Princess and Curdie* people are treated much more as types of different moral and civic behavior. In the latter book genuine interactions of characters are rare: Curdie, for instance, is much more formal in his relation to Irene's "grandmother." Then, in *The Princess and the Goblin*, we stay in one place: in *The Princess and Curdie*, we travel from one place to another.[2] Indeed, in *The Princess and the Goblin,* one of the central values is keeping to your place, which it is the central aim of the goblins to violate. So as we saw, Irene learns to be more fully the princess she is, Lootie the nurse is condemned for her presumption, and at the end Curdie chooses to remain a miner with his parents rather than accept a post at court. Even the goblins are obsessed with maintaining their toe-less racial distinction. But in *The Princess and*

---

2. One critic has called *The Princess and the Goblin* feminine and *The Princess and Curdie*, with its linear movement, masculine: Patterson, "Kore Motifs in *The Princess and the Goblin*," 170.

Curdie there is often no "place": Curdie turns out to have royal blood; a man may have a beast inside him, or a beast a man; and a human city may be invaded by creatures from purgatory. Here the walls of being are much thinner, and identity is less stable. There is more mixing of contexts: Curdie travels to the city and the royal palace; the mystic grandmother is found in the mines as much as in her attics, and she herself travels to the city to rescue the king.

This instability is conveyed through the theme of change. By contrast, as we saw, *The Princess and the Goblin* was concerned with space—the relations of the goblin and human mines, the different levels of the castle, the constriction of the goblin tunnels, the increasing expansion of grandmother's domain, the gradual movement inwards towards Princess Irene. *The Princess and Curdie*, however, is pervaded rather by time. The book opens with the making of a mountain that, in growing harmony with nature and humanity, contributes to the wealth and happiness of the world. This gives the perspective of aeons to the human story. We are introduced to fifty grotesque creatures who are former wicked humans undergoing spiritual growth through degradation and labor on behalf of good: this conveys a sense of a larger world of evolution around the narrative. And we find humans also changed and changing. Curdie has grown into a materialist youth who rejects the unseen, and has to be changed back to moral health by Irene's "grandmother." The king himself, once so powerful, is now a sick and bedridden old man being slowly poisoned by his counsellors. Though he is in the end rescued and restored to power, he soon dies, and the kingdom finally slips into the hands of a greedy tyrant, whose reckless mining for gold beneath Gwyntystorm brings about the city's and his own ruin.

When we consider this and other differences, it is almost fair to say that in the scope and specificity of its contrasts *The Princess and Curdie* could be called the inverse reflection of *The Princess and the Goblin*. Taken together, the two are opposite faces of one coin.

The difference-in-similarity between the two "Princess" books expresses an idea we see throughout *The Princess and Curdie*—that reality is as much discontinuous as a seamless whole. What looks the same is here also different. And this is in fact a major theme of the book, in which appearance and reality are rarely the same. Irene's grandmother tells Curdie that she can take any form and, in addition, that anyone who meets her sees his or her own subjective version of her. One night she appears to Curdie as a frail old crone, and on the next, in the mine, she is a beautiful young

The Princess and Curdie (1882)

woman: but her self within remains constant. She says, "'Shapes are only dresses, Curdie, and dresses are only names. That which is inside is the same all the time.'" When he asks, "'Then how can all the shapes speak the truth?'" she replies, "'It would want thousands more to speak the truth, Curdie; and then they could not.'" She goes on,

> "But there is a point I must not let you mistake about. It is one thing the shape I choose to put on, and quite another the shape that foolish talk and nursery tale may please to put upon me. Also, it is one thing what you or your father may think about me, and quite another what a foolish or bad man may see in me. For instance, if a thief were to come in here just now, he would think he saw the demon of the mine, all in green flames, come to protect her treasure, and would run like a hunted wild goat. I should be all the same, but his evil eyes would see me as I was not."[3] (55)

Here we change what we see by the light of our varying inner selves. This is what happens to Curdie as he grows in belief in the lady: first he could not see her (26), then he saw her as a very frail, wispy, almost spider-like old lady (27–28), then as "a tall, strong woman, plainly very old, but as grand as she was old" (33), and later, in the mines and on his second visit to the attics, as a beautiful, and each time younger, woman (48–49, 66). Our imaginations form pictures of reality according to our inner spiritual states. If we do not believe in "spirit" at all, but only in matter, then we see nothing.

This idea of dual selves and changing appearances was also present in *The Princess and the Goblin*, when Irene first met her grandmother as an old lady, but then, as her belief in the lady grew, as a progressively younger and more grand woman. And later, Curdie cannot see the grandmother at all because he does not believe in her or anything beyond the material world. But *The Princess and the Goblin* was much more concerned with the idea of belief in the unseen than it was with the theme of appearance versus reality. Grandmother was always present in the meanest image of her: only she revealed more of herself as the person seeing her grew in belief. But in *The Princess and Curdie*, we have people who hide their true selves from the view of others. Even grandmother can now become a false picture of herself when she appears as a demon of the mine to a wicked miner.

The theme of appearance versus reality is occasionally to be seen elsewhere in MacDonald's fantasy, but to a lesser extent, because *The Princess*

---

3. MacDonald, *The Princess and the Goblin and The Princess and Curdie*, ed. McGillis, 209. References are to this edition.

and Curdie is the only fantasy of his in which things are continually hidden. In *Phantastes*, Anodos is at one point tricked by the Alder Maiden's likeness to his white lady; in *Lilith*, both Lilith and Mara frequently change into leopards, while Lilith deceives Vane; and in "The Golden Key," the three Old Men are progressively younger, the third being a baby. Nearer is *At the Back of the North Wind*, where the great lady of the sky tells little Diamond that "'I have to shape myself various ways to various people'";[4] and she also grows big or small depending on her strength. On one occasion, she takes the form of a wolf to terrify a drunken nurse who is neglecting her charge; on another she plays with Diamond by assuming a whole variety of shapes.[5] She tells Diamond that he only sees her as a beautiful woman because he himself is good; and insists that, however much her appearance changes, her inside self remains the same.[6] But this theme is not so dominant as it is in *The Princess and Curdie*. And in the latter book, it is also applied to the false appearances human beings can assume for the purpose of deception.

In *The Princess and Curdie*, true reality is always under the surface, whether it is the child soul beneath the hideous shape of Lina, the vulture inside the human body of the lord chamberlain, the heart beneath the shifting appearances of the great lady Irene, the gold beneath the mountain and the city. Mining to dig out the hidden is a central motif of the book, and, like Curdie's hands, is an image for the seeing imagination. Ordinary human perception in *The Princess and Curdie* seems often ill-equipped to discover the true nature of the world, and it takes Curdie's magic "seeing hands" to be certain of the true nature of those he meets. This gives the book a tone of darkness: however vigilant we may be, it seems to say, nothing short of magic will enable us to see through hypocrisy. However, deception sometimes exposes itself unawares. When Curdie digs his way into the king's cellars, it is to see a palace servant putting something suspicious into the wine intended for the king. Of course, being in the cellars at all may be an image of Curdie's having penetrated by digging and mining beneath the surface to the truth under the hypocrisies of the court: but since he has not had to use his "seeing hands" to perceive the truth here, we are less likely to read this way.

At the court, the counsellors about the king pretend concern for him while slowly poisoning him; and at the same time they are hidden from

---

4. MacDonald, *At the Back of the North Wind*, 289.
5. MacDonald, *At the Back of the North Wind*, 68–69, 129–30.
6. MacDonald, *At the Back of the North Wind*, 92–94, 288–89.

themselves, for unknown to them their hypocrisy is turning their own inner natures to vicious bestial forms below the human. Princess Irene, caring for her father, thinks nothing but good of the evil Dr Kelman until Curdie enlightens her; and the king has been drugged into compliance. This is an environment in which the notion of "good" itself has been perverted: the first priest of Gwyntystorm delivers a sermon saying it is good is to give away one's superfluities to one's needy neighbors because that makes the giver more pleased with himself (315). One senses MacDonald making a side-swipe at elements in Victorian charity here.

Elsewhere too, *The Princess and Curdie* is full of uncertainties about identity. Early in the story our fairly happy picture of the house where young Irene lived in *The Princess and the Goblin* is rudely shaken, when we find the place now ruled by a hostile and snobbish housekeeper and a number of morally dubious servants. A green light Curdie and his father see one night in the mines leads them far into unknown regions: it could be a deception, but in the end it turns into a strange woman's face near them, which Curdie only at length recognizes by the eyes to be a form of the lady of the attics. It is not clear whether we are to consider Curdie's mother and father as country folk privileged by being poor or as potential royalty (207–8, 340). The city of Gwntystorm becomes uncertain in nature when Lina and the forty-nine strange creatures from the forest enter it, for it is inhabited at once by living humans and by creatures from purgatory.

Indeed, our first vision of Gwyntystorm is confused, for we are given two different pictures of it. Initially, it strikes Curdie as a place of wild grandeur, "a great rock in the river, which dividing flowed around it, and on the top of the rock the city, with lofty walls and towers and battlements, and above the city the palace of the king, built like a strong castle" (240). However, the next sentence goes on, "But the fortifications had long been neglected." This could be part of the theme of imaginative sight piercing through shows to discover dingy truths behind facades: but the emphasis here is more on what is seen than the eyes—or even hands—perceiving it. A similar "double-take" occurs to Curdie in the next paragraph when he gets close to "the mighty rock, which sparkled all over with crystals," and finds "a narrow bridge defended by gates and portcullis and towers with loopholes": but then he sees that "the gates stood wide open, and were dropping from their great hinges; the portcullis was eaten away with rust, and clung to the grooves evidently immovable; while the loopholed towers had neither floor nor roof, and their tops were fast filling up their interiors" (240–41).

The nature of the king Curdie then meets becomes indefinite too: for we find the hearty, outgoing, and confident ruler of *The Princess and the Goblin* now abruptly replaced by a bedridden and petulant old man. Where we had a sick mother in the first book, now we have a sick father.[7] Curdie cannot take in the change, finding the king's voice "altogether unlike what he remembered of the mighty, noble king on his white horse" (268). Nothing has prepared us for this alteration, for even at the beginning of this book we were still being told of the king using the wealth gathered from the mine wisely: "He was a real king—that is one who ruled for the good of his people, and not to please himself, and he wanted the silver . . . to help him to govern the country" (175). We are also told that he used it to pay his armies to defend the country and "the judges whom he set to portion out righteousness among the people, that so they might learn it themselves, and come to do without judges at all" (175–76). All this portrays a sort of utopia of good governance, so that when we arrive at the decrepit capital city, experience the selfishness of the populace, and find the army, judiciary, and all civil functions all poisoned by the greed and treachery of their officers, we wonder if we are in the same story. One picture has been changed for another. It is as though Curdie's truth-seeing hands have been applied to everything he sees in Gwyntystorm, not just to handshakes with dubious characters.

A similar gulf between our previous knowledge and present reality is seen between Princess Irene's last appearance in *The Princess and the Goblin* as still a delightful nine-year-old child, and the now much taller and older-looking figure that comes to greet Curdie in the dimly lit king's chamber (267). He recognizes her through her behavior more than her appearance; and we too take a while to accept that this figure is still the girl we knew in *The Princess and the Goblin*. Meanwhile, such is the obscurity in the king's chamber that Irene has to come right up to Curdie to be sure of who he is. And as observed, the princess has none of the vitality she possessed in the earlier book;[8] Curdie spends far more time with old Queen Irene, in her

---

7. Joseph Sigman, "The Diamond in the Ashes," 184, sees this as defining the themes of the two books, in the first of which the unconscious is sick and in the second the social and outside world.

8. Patterson, "Kore Motifs in *The Princess and the Goblin*," 187, sees her as "reduced to a very minor character."

The Princess and Curdie (1882)

various forms, than he does with the young princess he so often met in the earlier book.

The world itself with which we are dealing also becomes uncertain in nature. For one thing, there are at least two worlds, that of the country and that of the city. And now, as well as a boy with seeing hands, we have fifty animals impossible to nature, from a creature shaped like a sphere to a winged serpent that walks on tiny legs; and at the head of them all, the fantastic and hideous assemblage that is the dog Lina. These creatures from purgatory translate the local doings of the citizens into acts that will determine their fates beyond death.

The book itself falls into two parts. The first third of it deals with the training of Curdie by the lady, while the remainder portrays Curdie's doings in Gwyntystorm. The first part is set in the country and has an individual emphasis; the second has an urban and social concern. The one portrays a process of spiritual evolution in Curdie, whereby he learns to trust beyond his senses, and to believe in the unseen. The other shows us the decline of Gwyntystorm, the decay of social bonds, and spiritual descent in the form of the beasts the citizens are becoming. The two sections are also made discontinuous because no clear purpose arises from Curdie's early education. For much of his time with the lady it seems he is being made better for his own sake, because of his previous moral indifference. But then at the end she tells him he must travel to Gwyntystorm; and even then she will not say why (224–25). This leaves us to surmise that Curdie is simply going to the king's court because he is now morally fit to join it. It is only later that we can look back and say that the lady was preparing Curdie for a particular task in the city (275). But the fact that she will not vouchsafe it means that Curdie and we have to begin what seems an entirely new story when he leaves her.

The two sections of the book are also divided as "inside" and "outside." At first, we deal with the inner world, the world of the spirit and imagination. When Curdie becomes agonized at having shot the lady's bird, "the underground waters gushed from the boy's heart" (182). When he goes to own up to the lady, and finds her room full of moonlight, he wonders, "'But there's no moon outside,'" to which she replies, "'Ah! but you're inside now'" (187). We are prepared for this by the way Curdie finds the lady's elusive attic rooms in the big house: "He knew its outside perfectly, and now his business was to get his notion of the inside right with the outside"—

> So he shut his eyes and made a picture of the outside of it in his mind. Then he came in at the door of the picture, and yet kept the picture before him all the time—for you can do that kind of thing in your mind—and took every turn of the stair over again, always watching to remember, every time he turned his face, how the tower lay, and then when he came to himself at the top where he stood, he knew exactly where it was, and walked at once in the right direction. (185)

The idea of insides and outsides, and the relation between them, is to be the subject of much of the lady's later discourse to Curdie. In this first part of the book, the door of the big house is always open, despite the housekeeper's efforts, signifying the way inside; but in the second half, doors are generally closed, conveying exclusion, and to pass through them they have to be broken. The ruined gate of Gwyntystorm is left open, but this is a sign of indifference to the outside world, not of welcome; on entering the city and being met with hostility, Curdie tells Lina, "'the people keep their gates open, but their houses and their hearts shut'" (247).

In the first part of the book, Curdie learns to value the inside world of the imagination more than the outer world. From believing only in material things—so much that he was approaching the position of a man for whom "to be sure of a thing . . . [was] to have it between his teeth" (180)—Curdie learns to believe in the real existence of the mystic lady in the attics, and to have faith in her while she is absent from him in the mines. In other words, his imagination starts to revive. There too, he is shown how, by the light of the lady, beautiful ores and gems reveal themselves, as they do not in ordinary light (204–5). This is the operation of the imagination that shows the true beauty in ordinary things. When Curdie puts his hands in the lady's strange rose fire, he feels spiritual pain physically; but when the pain stops, not only are his hands changed, but so is his imagination. The rose fire is God's love, which expresses itself as burning only when we are not at one with it.[9] After Curdie has kept his hands in the fire, the pain disappears, and he is in harmony with the spiritual current of the universe.

Given Curdie's mystic training by Queen Irene, we might expect that his sojourn in Gwyntystorm would be directed at matters of the imagination and the unseen. Perhaps the grotesque creatures, in themselves terrifying, could have accomplished wonders that might have begun to move the souls of the inhabitants, while Curdie himself called them to repentance.

---

9. MacDonald, "The Consuming Fire," *Unspoken Sermons*, 18–33.

But, counter to MacDonald's usually generous theology, most of the citizens are judged out of hand as irredeemable, and the only objective is their exposure and punishment. The wills of the people are considered incorrigible. Because of this, we find that the next two thirds of the book are almost exclusively "physical" in emphasis. Like Curdie himself, the spiritual world goes underground, and materialism appears to dominate.

Everything we come across at first is the mutual impact of solids. Curdie's first encounter in Gwyntystorm is with a baker, who has just fallen over a piece of rock sticking up in the street and hurt his head. The rock is then levelled by Curdie's mattock, but fragments of it break the barber's window. Then the butcher's dogs attack Curdie and Lina, and are killed, one with Curdie's pickaxe through its brain, the other with its neck snapped in half in Lina's jaws. Thrown in a dungeon by the citizenry, Curdie hacks his way at a weak part of the stone floor, helped by the light thrown by Lina's great eyes, until he breaks through and sees water far below. The method by which he then gets himself through this hole, finds a rough passage leading off just below it, and manoeuvres himself and Lina into it, is all so detailed at the physical and practical level that we seem to be dealing simply with the movement of bodies. The same seems true later when the fantastic beasts also arrive in Curdie's former dungeon room, and the legserpent stretches itself from the hole to the passage, so that the other creatures may use his body as a bridge.

The eventual punishments of the wicked people of the palace are entirely physical—the doctor has his leg bitten through, the legserpent bites the lord chamberlain's nose and reshapes his silver bed into a cage, the attorney-general is wrapped in a cocoon of spider-web, a gluttonous magistrate is given a bath in his own turtle soup. The beasts also visit the dirty and insanitary castle kitchens to give the corrupt servants a physical taste of their own bad medicine.

Meanwhile, the imaginative insight embodied in Curdie's transformed hands is not always needed to determine the spiritual nature of a person. We have seen how the servant in the palace cellar is found by Curdie in the act of pouring a liquid into the king's wine. Curdie sees with his own natural eyes that something is wrong, and this is later confirmed. Then he is told by Princess Irene that the sick king's doctor, Kelman ("Kill-man"), whom she likes and trusts, administers this wine to him as medicine; but the king has been ill for a year and is now worse. Curdie therefore suspects Dr Kelman before meeting him. When the doctor arrives, and trips over on the way in, Curdie offers him a hand up, and finds himself grasping "the belly of a creeping thing" (271). Next morning, when we first meet the lord chamberlain, he and his actions are so described as to indicate wickedness—he looks, with his thin hook nose, glittering eyes, long scraggy neck, and lean, yellow aspect, very like the vulture Curdie's hand is later to find he is inside (283, 293). By this point, Curdie has begun to suspect a wider plot against the king, and his hand is needed only to confirm this. Metaphysics is thus not so much a determinant in the plot as might have been expected.

There is also a question concerning the recovery of the king. The good bread and wine Curdie and Irene feed him set him on the road to recovery from what has been portrayed as a physical illness. But then, one night, Curdie finds the king laid in a bed of burning roses by the great lady of the attics, after enduring which, "The king opened his eyes, and the soul of perfect health shone out of them" (328). Clearly the lady's ministrations are meant to provide the purgation of his spirit, yet, coming out of nowhere as they do, they seem as much a garnish to his physical cure. And at the end of the story, when the lady uses her doves as missiles against the invading army, we feel partly that creatures of spiritual import have been reduced to material weapons.

Of course, it will be replied, we are not to read these actions as merely physical. The doves are in part divine grace and love, which their enemies cannot bear, being at a distance from them (compare MacDonald, "It is only at a distance it [divine love] burns"[10]). The king's sickness, it may be argued, is not finally physical at all: he says once that he fell sick at the degeneration of his subjects (290). It could, on the other hand, be posited that the king's sickness and poisoning represent an illness of his soul, which has sent evil to all his members, the people of his country. However, MacDonald is unwilling to show his king as at all spiritually wrong, so that any such metaphoric reading goes against the literal one given.[11] His emphasis, moreover, is not on the king's sickness but on his being poisoned by others. It seems not insignificant that MacDonald's essay "The Elder Hamlet" appeared just before the serialization of this story.[12]

10. MacDonald, *Unspoken Sermons*, 319.

11. Osama Jarrar, "Language, Ideology and Fairy Tales," 141–42, comes close to this view, which implicates the king in the failure of his subjects, before choosing the more evident fact that he is too sick and weak to act against the evil: "the kingdom is no longer stable because the king is physically and psychologically unstable: the king cannot get rid of the wicked people" (ibid., 42).

12. There are remarkable similarities between *The Princess and Curdie* and *Hamlet*. A

The Princess and Curdie (1882)

We can more readily argue that the king has been cut off from his subjects in Gwyntystorm just as his spirit has been cut off from his body—his mind wandering, his body poisoned. Also, when Curdie enters Gwyntystorm, this could be a figure for entering the king's self, his limbs. When he has his debate with the baker about who was responsible for the obstructive stone in the king's highway, the baker blames the king for not removing the stone, but Curdie says that the baker's "king," his head, should have guided his feet (242). This idea of "man the microcosm" is one native to Shakespeare: and this scene also has suggestive parallels in *Henry V* (the debate before Agincourt on the king's responsibility for his subjects' deaths in battle, IV, i, 86–280) and in *Coriolanus* (Menenius' speech condemning the rebellious members of the civil body, I, i, 94–152). The potential medical analogy throughout Curdie's workings in the city is with a vaccine or antibiotic that enters the body and removes the disease that inhabits it: the wicked are in the end purged like bacteria. However, we are still dealing here with order in the body politic, not with the metaphysics of the imagination.

Inside the palace Curdie finds its officers idle or in revolt, and the sources of their food, the kitchens, dirty and unhealthy. All the passages and rooms he visits could be seen as metaphors for parts of the king's brain. By investigating them all, Curdie makes connections concerning what is going on, and draws everything together into a plan of action. What was secret or divided from others is pulled into one; and in parallel the discomposed mind and the sick body of the king become once more coherent. The king himself can also be seen as having become separated from the divine source of his being: then the good bread and wine he is fed become symbols of renewed communion, and the lady completes his restoration through the rose fire that burns away all remaining distance from God's love.

All this may doubtless have some truth, and perhaps MacDonald intended that the physical actions, items, and characters should so operate as metaphors of the spirit and its changes. Perhaps when we read how, after the punishment of the slovenly kitchen servants, "there was such a cleaning and clearing out of neglected places, such a burying and burning

---

young man is given a task by a supernatural figure. The world he encounters in Gwyntystorm is one in which appearances mask reality, and people plot to undermine one another. The spiritual world goes underground, and the world seems merely physical and corrupting, the "too too solid flesh" defeating mental life. The poisoning of the king poisons the whole of society: something is rotten throughout Gwyntystorm and the country, as in Denmark.

of refuse, such a rinsing of jugs, such a swilling of sinks, and such a flushing of drains, as would have delighted the eyes of all true housekeepers and lovers of cleanliness generally" (309)—perhaps we should be reading this as a metaphor for the king's renewed self: but the sheer physical detail and specificity tend to suppress such a reading. And so it is with all the other too, too solid descriptions, from the movements of Curdie into and through the palace to the bizarre punishments meted out by the fantastic beasts to the counsellors.

As for the beasts themselves, collectively they could be said to be an image of the monsters that rise from a sick imagination, whether "the terrible dreams" of the king himself or the putative guilts of the evil servants. Lina passes among the servants "like a shapeless terror through a guilty mind" (281); and occasionally we are told that the strange forms of the creatures express some previous distortion of the soul, as with Curdie's reflection on "Ballbody" (309). But usually the mental and spiritual aspects are lost in their more practical uses as hole-borers, bridges, trippers-up, and tormentors.

There was something of the same duality of spirit and matter that we find in this book in *The Princess and the Goblin*. On the one hand, we had the mystical realm of the old princess at the top of the house, where every solid-seeming object, from a bath to a fire, and from a dove to a spinning wheel, was also a Christian symbol; and, on the other hand, we were with the very practical operations of Curdie against the goblins in and around the mines. But this duality was overcome by the overarching symbolism of the mind in the landscape of the book—attics, day-rooms, mines (imagination, reason plus the senses, the "dark" unconscious). It was further overcome in the way that each "spiritual" and mystical chapter alternated with one concerning Curdie and the more physical world, so that the two were not divided, but became aspects of one another. (There is a similar treatment in *At the Back of the North Wind*.) But in *The Princess and Curdie* the two areas are more radically separated.

Why are there all these dualities in *The Princess and Curdie*? The explanation may lie in a theme that runs throughout. It is sounded from the first chapter, in which there is the strange and moving picture of the birth of the mineral-rich mountain from the fiery depths of the earth. This mountain is described, in no mere personification, as "the heart of the earth . . . come rushing up among her children, bringing with it gifts of all that she possesses" (175): the mountain's wealth is freely given. Life then partly colonizes the outside of the mountain, before humans come to dig shafts and tunnels into it to mine its ores. In the hands of a wise king, these riches are used to sustain the offices of a healthy kingdom. Like mountain streams that end in the ocean, thence to return once more to the mountain as rain, wealth flows from the center to the furthest and poorest in the land, and is returned in work, productivity, and social happiness. But when people dammed this flow, and seized the wealth for themselves, "then it grew diseased and was called *mammon*" (176). They hid this wealth away. This is the opposite of what miners do: the business of Curdie and his father "was to bring to light hidden things" (175). This is later to be true in another sense, when Curdie mines his way into and through the palace of Gwyntystorm to expose the evil and bring the hidden king to light.

The people of Gwyntystorm keep things, and themselves, to themselves. They stop them moving and circulating.[13] When Curdie picks up the stone in the Gwyntystorm street, the barber demands it from him, not because he wants it for itself, but merely to have power over it (243). Because the people care only for themselves and what they may possess, all social sense has declined in them, and their city, for all the wealth it contains, appears ruinous. The barber cares nothing for the injured head of his "friend" the baker, only for the damage Curdie has accidentally caused to his window; the butcher is outraged that Curdie has killed his dog when it tried to kill him first; the magistrate waits till he has had his second breakfast before proceeding with Curdie's trial: everywhere material or bestial values are put above human or civil ones—everywhere, that is, save in the baker's wife and the poor old woman Derba, who give Curdie good bread and hospitality. The imagination that makes love and society possible is absent.

These city people do not care even for their own past, thinking their present far superior to anything before (241): they shut themselves off in time just as they shut themselves off socially. They think of the king only as bound to take care of them, as each takes care of him- or herself (242); and they care so little about him that they do not notice that they have not seen him for some time. They are so wrapped up in themselves that none of them has noticed, as Curdie does, that the very rock of the city streets is impregnated with gold (287–88). Their selfishness is epitomized as we saw in their good works, which involve giving to the needy only so much superfluity as will swell the complacency of the giver. For the "first

---

13. Osama Jarrar, "Children's Fiction Discourse Analysis," 58–59, also makes this point concerning the analogy between the mountain and human society.

fundamental principle, grounded in inborn invariable instinct, was, that every One should take care of that One. This was the first duty of Man" (315). The mountain, we recall, gave its wealth to all, as once did the king. But the greed of the people has made them foolish enough to believe that they need not pay to mend the city's defences, because they can hide their gold from an invader: they think to save their money by putting it at risk (324). Far from their owning their wealth, it owns them.

As for the people within the palace, the king's counsellors are busily trying to weaken his mind so much that he will sign away the kingdom to them; and the servants have neglected their work for eating, drinking, and thieving. The counsellors are simply higher class robbers: on the night of their eventual punishment, the lord chamberlain is in his bed of silver gilt, and the attorney general is "trying the effect of a diamond star which he had that morning taken from the jewel-room" (312). After vengeance is exercised on them, they are all ironically driven to huddle together for the night in the tiny hovel of Derba, the only person in the city who will give them shelter.

The implications of such materialism are outlined by MacDonald in his Platonic "unspoken" sermon, "The Hardness of the Way":

> Things are given us, this body first of things, that through them we may be trained both to independence and true possession of them. We must possess them; they must not possess us. Their use is to mediate—as shapes and manifestations in lower kind of the things that are unseen, that is, in themselves unseeable, the things that belong, not to the world of speech, but the world of silence, not to the world of showing but the world of being, the world that cannot be shaken, and must remain. These things unseen take form in the things of time and space—not that they may exist, for they exist in and from eternal Godhead, but that their being may be known by those in training for the eternal; these things unseen the sons and daughters of God must possess. But instead of reaching out after them, they grasp at their forms, reward the things seen as the things to be possessed, fall in love with the bodies instead of the souls of them.[14]

Putting material things first, the evil people of Gwyntystorm live in a world of nothing but matter. Their wealth contrasts with the huge emerald the lady seizes from the floor of the mine and gives to Curdie's father: while Curdie is on his quest it will stay green when things go well with

---

14. MacDonald, *Unspoken Sermons*, 200.

him, but will turn pale when they do not; here the stone's power is changed from mercantile to metaphysical, from getting to giving. By contrast, the obstructive stone that Curdie dislodges from the street in Gwntystorm is immediately coveted by the barber even though it is valueless to him.

The mountain described at the beginning of the book symbolizes a condition of sharing, of the ceaseless creation of God that is forever changing to new forms. The people of Gwyntystorm refuse such community, have no bonds with one another. Shut up in themselves as they are, they are not open to any change or influence from outside. The lust for things in Gwyntystorm separates the book into its two sections, the first dealing with the now more isolated spiritual and imaginative realm of the lady, and the second concerned with the material and materialistic world the city has become. Rightfully governed, the city should shadow a heavenly one, but Gwyntystorm/Jerusalem has become more a Babylon or even a Gomorrah.[15] Similarly, the physical appearance of a human or a beast has become divorced from its inner nature. Those who look like humans may in fact be snakes or vultures, and those with the aspects of hideous creatures may have human and gentle inner selves. Because appearance is no longer an index to reality, because the physical and the spiritual no longer mirror one another, what we see becomes uncertain in nature. We see a noble and then a weak king, a government first apparently ideal, then corrupt, a city that, as Curdie approaches it, changes from imposing nobility to ruinous decrepitude. Lina the dog is here a symbol, for her body is a composite of many ill-suited identities, none of which expresses the present nature of her inside self.

Here again the mountain supplies a template, for it unites opposites in itself. For first, it is both still and moving. It is formed out of liquid fire, cools to an apparent solid, yet then lives among the winds, the rains, and the suns, sustaining life in grass, beasts, and humans, freezing water into glaciers, and releasing it as streams. It is like a living body, which is also part of the larger body of the world, and its water

> runs in channels as the blood in the body: little veins bring it down from the ice above into the great caverns of the mountain's heart, whence the arteries let it out again, gushing in pipes and clefts and ducts of all shapes and kinds, through and through its bulk, until it springs newborn to the light, and rushes down the mountain in

---

15. Willis, *The Downstretched Hand*, 186–87, 190, draws the close parallel here with the description of doomed Babylon in Revelation 15.

torrents, and down the valleys in rivers—down, down, rejoicing, to the mighty lungs of the world, that is the sea, where it is tossed in storms and cyclones, heaved up in billows, twisted in waterspouts, dashed to mist upon rocks, beaten by millions of tails, and breathed by millions of gills, whence at last, melted into vapour by the sun, it is lifted up pure into the air, and borne by the servant winds back to the mountaintops and the snow, the solid ice, and the molten stream. (175)

The water here is a figure of the imagination itself, filling the world with spirit. And the mountain is part of the family of the universe, not something cut off, like a miser with his wealth. The sun is its "grandfather" and the moon its "little old cold aunt," and the wind turns the rocks and caverns "into a roaring organ for the young archangels that are studying how to let out the pent-up praises of their hearts" (174). This is the world of the creative imagination founded in God. Here the "material" and the "spiritual" are one, for the mountain is a gift from the heart of mother earth to her children, and the creatures of heaven delight in it. Its inside is as rich as its exterior, and there is no divorce between outer and inner worlds. It is at once a center, for beasts, humans, and archangels come to it; and a periphery, for it is but a bubble sent up by the earth, itself once a mere blot of fire thrown out by the sun. It is hot and cold, darkness and light, solitude and society, all together. It even unites opposite impressions in the beholder:

> A mountain is a strange and awful thing. In old times, without knowing so much of their strangeness and awfulness as we do, people were yet more afraid of mountains. But then somehow they had not come to see how beautiful they are as well as awful, and they hated them—and what people hate they must fear. Now that we have learned to look at them with admiration, perhaps we do not always feel quite awe enough of them. To me they are beautiful terrors. (9)

Within the book itself, such a reconciliation of contraries is possible only occasionally, with the mystic Queen Irene, who we are told is both old and young (192, 207, 210, 216), and who heals the king with both fire and water (326-27).

Just as the book began with a prologue describing events from the very beginning before its narrative, so in an epilogue it pursues things to their very end. (One commentator has even seen the story as canvassing the whole of earth's history, from genesis to apocalypse, from the rocks of the beginning to the human-free world of its end.[16]) Gwyntystorm, which in its once better state was a civility married to nature, a town on a rock in a river, is now a collection of shapeless boulders in the midst of a nature that, on its own, is much more savage. Gwyntystorm has reverted to what its name means in Welsh—"a storm of winds."

If *The Princess and the Goblin* may be viewed as humankind in an early phase of self-definition, then *The Princess and Curdie* marks the opposite, the end-time, the coming of judgment and the destruction of the world. Here the very energy that has propelled humanity's development becomes its poison, and erases it from the book of life. And as it does so, humanity's inner nature, so determinedly evolutionary, reverts once more to the brutish form from which it thought it had clambered, taking on the lineaments of snake, vulture, or toad. Thus, the optimistic, spring-like, dilating mode of *The Princess and the Goblin* shifts to the more contractile mode of *The Princess and Curdie*, where we go into a rotting city that stands on steadily shrinking supports, governed by a sick king and a diseased court and focused on an ever-grasping hand. Thus seen, the two books form a diptych, in which the very expansive, self-defining impulse of the one becomes the self-destruction of the other.

And on the evidence, the world of the imagination and the spirit can do nothing lasting on earth to avert the end. Although we have a sense of providence at work in the world, in the shapes of the great lady and her birds, the strange beasts whose past evils are working themselves out, the fire of roses that gives Curdie spiritual insight beyond his natural means, and heals the ruined nature of a king, all these things ultimately fail to check human wickedness. And it may be noted that this is not simply the fault of the evil forces: there is something lacking in King Curdie's encouragement of the citizens of Gwyntystorm to dig into the foundations of their city for gold; something missing in a king who, though victorious against his enemies, remains at odds with his own people; something a little more than unfortunate in the lack of royal children that allows tyranny to take over after the deaths of Curdie and Irene.

The accent in this book is, in the end, more on quitting the world than on staying in it. Irene, Curdie, the good king, Lina, and the strange gang of beasts, have all left the stage of life. The motif of old age has run through the story, from the oft-mentioned insubstantiality of old Queen Irene, to

---

16. Sundmark, "Travelling Beastward," 7–8.

Curdie's elderly father and mother and the fading condition of the king. When Curdie crosses the evil heathland on his way to Gwyntystorm, he sits down under a lone hawthorn, "very old and distorted. . . . It looked so like a human being dried up and distorted with age and suffering" (231). This recalls Queen Irene's appearance as a "withered bracken bush" to one of the miners' wives earlier (200); and the frequent occurrence of the word "withered" in relation to her (187, 192, 196, 198). Of course, her equal youth and strength are also insisted upon, but this does not supersede the sense of frailty and age, as it does in *The Princess and the Goblin,* where, as the Princess comes to see her great grandmother more clearly, she appears younger.

On the heath, the landscape and the hawthorn "were so withered that it was impossible to say whether they were alive or not." Then, while the sun is "going down in a storm of crimson," there gets up from the west a strange wind "that felt red and hot the one moment, and cold and pale the other. It seemed to come from the deathbed of the sun, dying in fever and ague" (232). This is a vision of the end of things, out of which comes the grotesque dog Lina, a creature from another world. It is images like these that spread entropy and apocalypse in the story, and take us back to the song of the lady Irene during Curdie's last interview with her.

> The stars are spinning their threads,
> And the clouds are the dust that flies,
> And the suns are weaving them up
> For the time when the sleepers shall rise.
> . . .
> The weepers are learning to smile,
> And laughter to glean the sighs;
> Burn and bury the care and guile,
> For the day when the sleepers shall rise. (217)

In the very end, *The Princess and Curdie* looks away from the tangled world to the happier mercies of eternity. This movement is extended in MacDonald's next and last major fantasy *Lilith,* where the setting is purgatorial and the goal is heaven, to which MacDonald looked increasingly as his life waned.

7

Conclusion

It is sometimes assumed that MacDonald's view of the imagination is close to that of Coleridge. Coleridge actually distinguished two imaginations, the primary and the secondary. The primary imagination is the act of seeing itself, whereby, colored by our different subjectivities, the world appears to each of us uniquely: in this sense, to see is to create. "The primary imagination I hold to be the living power and prime agent of all human perception, and as a representation in the finite mind of the eternal act of creation in the infinite I AM." The secondary imagination, however, is concerned not with seeing so much as with doing. It takes the world perceived with the primary imagination and remakes it into something new: "It dissolves, diffuses, dissipates, in order to re-create."[1] An analogy might be melting down a saucepan to be remade as a cigar case: but this supposes that the basic constituents stay the same, where the secondary imagination has the more magical power of transforming, say, an apple to an angel. In fact, the process is akin to a deliberate dream. The highest product of the secondary imagination is, as Coleridge sees it, a philosophical poem, such as Wordsworth's *The Prelude*; but another mode in which this might appear would be the poetry of the supernatural, of which he himself has left us two striking examples, in *The Ancient Mariner* and "Kubla Khan." In the former, he renders down and remakes the many eighteenth-century records of voyages to unknown lands into a poetic tale, both of a journey to a world of ice and of an inner voyage to the frozen regions of the soul. In the latter, he

---

1. Coleridge, *Biographia Literaria,* 167.

transforms all visions of eastern luxury into a fabulous landscape trembling on the edge of decadence and haunted by the roaring of the suppressed imagination beneath its fanciful pastoral contrivance.

This is not MacDonald's view of the imagination or its operation. In the first place, God is for him the great imaginer from whom we draw all our creative energy. Coleridge, Christian though he was, did not admit the deity into the workings of the human imagination, which for him operated *sui generis* and only by analogy with God's imagination—"as a representation in the finite mind of the eternal act of creation in the infinite I AM." MacDonald is indeed highly novel in his view of God sitting in the darkest depths of the human mind and sending up "wonderful gifts into the light of that understanding which is His candle." While many thinkers of the nineteenth century began to equate the imagination with the unconscious mind, and to consider the writer as being directed from a source over which there was little control, they rarely looked to a divine source for this inspiration, and still less did they place God within the human mind. Nearest to MacDonald is perhaps John Ruskin in *Modern Painters* (1843–60);[2] and the appearance a year before MacDonald's "The Imagination" (1867) of Eneas Streetland Dallas's *The Gay Science*, the first part of which is on the unconscious imagination, seems more than mere coincidence.

Moreover, unlike Coleridge, MacDonald does not, in his essay on the imagination, speak of that faculty remaking what it sees. Rather, he conceives of the artist as using the materials of a world created by God, which he must search to find the image that best conveys his thought. "If we . . . consider the so-called creative faculty in man, we will find that in no *primary* sense is this faculty creative. Indeed, a man is rather *being thought* than *thinking*, when a new thought arises in his mind."[3] Thus, where Coleridge emphasizes the power of the imagination in re-making the world outside it,

---

2. Part of Ruskin's concern throughout *Modern Painters* is to avoid the subjectivism of Romantics such as Wordsworth, who were inclined to read their emotional promptings as universal truths; and at the same time to avoid that pictorialism that places all truth in the faithful copy of the external world. Ruskin eventually asserted that symbolic and mythic utterance contained transcendental truths fed into what amounted to the unconscious mind. In this, he is close to MacDonald: but MacDonald chose to guarantee the visions of the unconscious imagination as truth by putting God himself in that place of possible delusion. MacDonald and Ruskin became friends in 1863, later more intimately for reasons other than metaphysical. Ruskin made a gift of *Modern Painters* to MacDonald in 1864 (Greville MacDonald, *George MacDonald and His Wife*, 329).

3. MacDonald, "The Imagination," *A Dish of Orts*, 4.

Conclusion

MacDonald sees it as seeking out something already given. Coleridge's view is the Romantic one; MacDonald's is that of a Christian mystic.

This is not to say that MacDonald always writes differently from Coleridge. The opening of his first romance *Phantastes* (1858) describes what looks exactly like a process of dissolving, diffusing, and dissipating in order to re-create: for as the protagonist Anodos awakes one morning, it is to find that all the furniture and decorations of his bedroom are reshaping themselves to form a glade, at which he rises and finds himself walking in Fairy Land. But such a dissolution and reconstitution, while it may express a process going on in Anodos's mind, whereby he leaves the physical world behind and enters his own unconscious, is not carried out by Anodos himself. The day before this he has met a fairy lady, who told him he would enter Fairy Land next day, and so he did. In other words, a supernatural being outside him has changed his life. This is Anodos "more being thought than thinking." And if we look at others of MacDonald's fantasies, we frequently find supernatural authority figures initiating and guiding the action—the strange Mr Raven in *Lilith*, who draws the protagonist Vane into the region of the seven dimensions, the grandmother figure in *The Princess and the Goblin* and *The Princess and Curdie*, who brings both Irene and Curdie to her, the old woman who abducts Rosamond and Agnes in *The Wise Woman*, the great lady of the wind who takes young Diamond out with her in *At the Back of the North Wind*, the shadows who come for Ralph Rinkelmann in "The Shadows," the lady who brings both Tangle and Mossy into fairyland in "The Golden Key." In each story, just as with Coleridge's idea of the imagination, the process involves entry into a world of the unconscious, a dissolution of the old self and the making of a new one. But this process is managed not by the self but by a power *beyond* it.

And this is the central fact about MacDonald's fairy tales, that most of them exist to further our knowledge of a wider supernatural world, both within and beyond ours, to which in our spiritual selves we most truly belong. The great ladies of the longer stories, North Wind, Irene's "grandmother," and the wise woman, point to a realm of divine reality that coexists with our own and gives us spiritual renewal. They are angels from a world beyond death where goodness will find joy and evil be purged. Irene in her grandmother's bottomless bath, Curdie grasping the paw of the hideous dog Lina and feeling the hand of a baby, Diamond in the land at the back of the North Wind, Agnes meeting her self inside the wise woman's magic sphere—all feel a wonderful and terrible reality that lives in life and beyond it. Such moments are the deepest parts of the stories in which they occur, so real that everything beside them feels weightless. MacDonald has written these stories simply to give supernatural joy: for his numinous women are there to tell us that all things will be everlastingly well—even if this does not always seem the case.

We have said much on the role of the imagination in MacDonald's fairy tales, but less on how inventive they are. In his first tale, "Cross Purposes," MacDonald uses the old idea of the abduction of mortals by fairies and the human wit employed to escape them, as seen in the traditional fairy tales "Thomas the Rhymer" and "Tam Lin," but completely transforms our notion of fairy land and glamour into a plastic world where everything is illusory and in constant change. Umbrellas become geese and hang themselves on trees, a stream flows over grass and flowers or climbs hills, a cat becomes a cat-a-mountain, a seeming abyss is only a step down. MacDonald's peers here are the German Romantic fairy-story writer E. T. A. Hoffmann of "The Golden Pot," Hans Christian Andersen, and Thackeray in *The Rose and the Ring*, though Hoffmann's metamorphoses are confined to plants and serpents, Andersen's idea of the evil mirror and the Snow Queen are stable conditions in his story, and the grotesque human shape-shifts in *The Rose and the Ring* are steadily moral as well as wildly comic—as with Jenkins Gruffanuff, the rude palace door-keeper, whom Fairy Blackstick transforms to a knocker: "He was from being *brazen, brass!*"[4] MacDonald's creativity is even more various—he invents a stone staircase that falls out of a cliff-face, a series of Old Men of the Sea, the Earth, and the Fire of whom the last and oldest of all is a baby, a princess who is made weightless, a dog made of discordant parts, a series of absurd-looking creatures from purgatory, a lamp that shines through walls, a bath that has no bottom, a wind that wants to be friends, a talking group of stained-glass apostles in a cathedral, an antechamber to heaven, a picture gallery that gives entry to different worlds, a sphere in which one meets one's soul.

MacDonald also has a way of inverting our assumptions, turning the perceptions of reason and common sense upside-down. The wind trying to get into Diamond's rickety bedroom in *At the Back of the North Wind* may remind us of the South-West Wind trying to gain entrance to the brothers' farmhouse in Ruskin's *The King of the Golden River*: but MacDonald's wind

---

4. Actually derived originally from Hoffmann's *The Golden Pot* (end of Second Vigil). Dickens also uses the image in *A Christmas Carol* (1843) when Marley's face appears to Scrooge on his door-knocker (Stave 1, 19–20).

Conclusion

is trying not to get *in* to Diamond's house but to get *out* of her own "house" in the sky. If we feel the discrepancy of her trying to get *out of* a bigger place (the wide world) into a much smaller one (Diamond's bedroom), we are led to realize that she is not so much trying to get into Diamond's bedroom as into his soul, which is far vaster than any physical world. In "The Golden Key," the Oldest Man of all, the Old Man of the Fire, is a little child. The wise woman's cottage is bigger inside than out; and one must knock to find the door. Grandmother in *The Princess and the Goblin* tells Princess Irene that "'No one ever gives anything to another properly and really without keeping it'" (121). In this paradoxical idiom much of MacDonald's fantasy exists, because it lives in the God-based imagination.

MacDonald's fairy tales offer more than most kinds of story a great range of ever-changing responses. Each is like a kind of literary rollercoaster, always throwing up some new surprise, and always moving and changing direction. A boy in London suddenly meets the North Wind; and throughout his life keeps having visions of other realities. The Day Boy Photogen and the Night Girl Nycteris find their worlds steadily being replaced by a much larger one. "The Light Princess" and "Cross Purposes" are full of the idea of different depths in life. Across the stories as a whole there is a cornucopia of different realities and situations, from the magical world of Fairyland to Victorian London, and from the house of a giant to a highland cottage with a stream running through it or a boy in bed above a stable.

Even the traditional fairy tale is more predictable than this: a queen has three chances to tell a goblin his name or she will lose her child ("Rumpelstiltskin"); three tasks must be done to gain a kingdom (d'Aulnoy,"The White Cat"); a wife has the run of all the rooms in her house save one ("Bluebeard"); a frog helps a princess fill a sieve with water for her wicked stepmother on three conditions ("The Well of the World's End"). But in MacDonald's tales there is no such patterning, and much less ability to see ahead. No sooner is Ralph Rinkelmann made King of the Fairies than he is taken up by the shadows, who vary in character from the fanciful to the deeply real. In "The Carasoyn," the tasks Colin must carry out to win the girl prove absurd, and even when he has her, the queen takes his own son instead, thus starting a new story. Curdie, in *The Princess and Curdie*, is not told why he must travel to Gwyntystorm; North Wind comes to Diamond at seeming random; and while she often visits him during the first part, she is largely absent from the rest.

Like his mentor Novalis, MacDonald indeed thinks of the fairy tale itself as working like an aeolian harp that the wind visits at random.[5] This is why many of his fairy tales have the form of dreams. They are narratives often full of hallucinatory images that stir us at profound levels.

Now this is something quite new in the writing of English fantasy. The Victorian fairy tales before MacDonald are generally written in one idiom or register. Ruskin's *The King of the Golden River* (1851) has moments of comedy in the grotesque appearance of the South-West Wind Esquire or the re-assemblage of the various limbs of the King of the Golden River after he has been melted in the fire, but is generally an imitation of Grimm with a serious moral. Thackeray's *The Rose and the Ring*, on the other hand, is simply an elaborate pantomime, absurdly comic, and comically moral, throughout. The fairy tales of Frances Browne's in her *Granny's Wonderful Chair* are all based on traditional fairy lore. MacDonald's fairy tales are actually closer to the shifting style of E. T. A. Hoffmann in "The Golden Pot" (1814); or to Carlyle's *Sartor Resartus* (1836), which celebrates through a wild and ever-changing narrative direction the wonder of a God-based universe in which "'all . . . works together with all; is borne forward on the bottomless, shoreless flood of Action, and lives through perpetual metamorphoses.'"[6]

In MacDonald's stories, the narrative is not always the only important thing. In *The Princess and the Goblin*, Irene's visits to her grandmother in the attics form islands of contemplation amidst the story of the goblin plot. The finding of a golden key by Mossy, and his search for the lock it fits, is behind "The Golden Key," but during the story the desire shifts to a strange land "'from whence the shadows fall'"; and thereafter the story divides into two and we follow the girl Tangle, who does not have the key, on a long seeming digression underground. In "The Light Princess," we are as much taken up with exploring the consequences of being light in both body and spirit as we are with the finding of a remedy. In *At the Back of the North Wind*, the wind comes intermittently to young Diamond, and in between he is doing different things. Further, North Wind comes often in the first part of the book, and then is absent for much of the second. And in *The Wise Woman*, we have two very different central figures taken at different points in the story from very different places: they shift location continually and do not meet till the end.

5. MacDonald, "The Fantastic Imagination," *A Dish of Orts*, 321.
6. Carlyle, *Sartor Resartus*, 56.

Conclusion

Compared to the traditional tale, MacDonald's stories have much that we might call irrelevance, but which is actually a means of slowing us down to look at what is passing. In "The Giant's Heart," the episodes with the various birds are largely beside the narrative point, but they take us to lives outside the story. To find some of the strange wine the fairy queen demands, Colin in "The Carasoyn" finds himself having to perform a number of seemingly pointless tasks that serve to reveal a wonderful supernatural world amid a barren moor. Much time is spent in "Cross Purposes" on the various illusions with which Richard and Alice are beset before these are dismissed as frauds; but in the interim we have been immersed in the glamour of faerie. *At the Back of the North Wind* is full of visions and poems that add nothing to any plot, but much to the sense of the world as founded in mystery.

To some extent, MacDonald's fairy tales are forms of showing more than telling. In *The Princess and the Goblin*, we have a gradually unfolding picture of the mind. Even the goblin plots are, in a sense, unimportant, for Curdie finds out what these people are about and is able to prepare for them. The things that matter are the great images—of the swarming great goblin hall, the endless dark tunnels of the mines, the attics of the old "grandmother" and her gradual change to a beautiful and majestic woman surrounded by moon and stars. *At the Back of the North Wind*, by contrast, is a picture of the nature of the outside world, with Diamond taken out of his bed to travel across London and later England and the sea to the North Pole, with North Wind all the time trying to explain how things work to all people's good; and then the book shows us a Victorian London that is penetrated by a spiritual world. *The Princess and Curdie* in a sense continues "Cross Purposes," for it is a picture of how people operate by appearances.

Some fantasies form a process of deepening revelation. "The Golden Key," for instance, takes us from this world to Fairy land and then to the land beyond death before Mossy and Tangle ascend the rainbow to the country from whence the shadows fall. A similar deepening sequence is seen in "The Light Princess," where "depth" itself has particular significance. Only at the end of *The Wise Woman* is the gruff old woman revealed by Rosamond's little moral victory as a beautiful woman, full of the wonder of the divine imagination. Other stories shift back and forth between this world and another, or between human and non-human figures, as when a great supernatural being surfaces in the narrative from time to time. Or again, the narrative has another story beneath it: for instance "The Light Princess" hints at the story of Christ's sacrifice and resurrection, *At the Back of the North Wind* follows a pattern of alchemical transformation, the myth of Persephone underlies *The Princess and the Goblin*, and the Greek Eirinyes or vengeance stalk behind the narrative of *The Princess and Curdie*. Such accompanying stories are no mere allegories, but show how the individual imagination can be a meeting place across time for all other imaginations, and a single story become many.

In this revelatory mode of gradually exposing deeper levels of truth, MacDonald's fairy tales are not unlike the late sixteenth- and early seventeenth-century masque, particularly those by Ben Jonson, and Milton's *Comus* (1634), the latter of which MacDonald loved for its portrayal of human virtue sustained by grace.[7] Often in MacDonald's stories there is actual imagery of penetration to reality, as with Princess Irene gradually seeing more of the true majesty and beauty of her grandmother, or Curdie learning to see beneath people's appearances, Tangle going to the heart of the world in "The Golden Key," Richard seeing through the illusions of the fairies in "Cross Purposes," Agnes in *The Wise Woman* being shown in the magic sphere the hideous inner self she nourishes, Diamond going through North Wind to reach the country at her back. In "Photogen and Nycteris," Nycteris emerges gradually to the true nature of light—and then beyond: "'who knows,'" Nycteris would say to Photogen, "'that, when we go out, we shall not go into a day as much greater than your day as your day is greater than my night?'"[8] In *At the Back of the North Wind*, North Wind hears through all the misery of the world a beautiful far-off song that is coming ever nearer. The old ladies of the "Princess" books and *The Wise Woman* become transfigured. These visions are what the stories are ultimately about: they are the deepest reality below the action.

Yet MacDonald is no facile mystic. The shorter fairy tales can have happy endings because the issues faced by their protagonists are not those of real life, nor are the evils they contain—usually produced by such social outsiders as witches, giants, or fickle fairy queens—to be taken wholly seriously. Such tales follow standard patterns of romance and myth, and are not to be seen in escapist terms: they follow a primal rhythm of the destruction of happiness followed by its return. Thus, the fairy tale witch who makes the almost unbelievable experiment of dividing Photogen and Nycteris from

---

7. Celia Catlett Anderson, "*The Golden Key*: Milton and MacDonald."

8. MacDonald, "The History of Photogen and Nycteris, a Day and Night Mährchen," in MacDonald, *The Complete Fairy Tales*, ed. Knoepflmacher, 341.

day and from night is overthrown and they are freed; or a prince prepared to give his life to save a princess subjected to an absurd curse is saved, and they are happily married. But in the world of poor Victorian London in *At the Back of the North Wind*, the reality of young Diamond's supernatural visions is questioned, and benign views of the workings of the universe are challenged. Elsewhere MacDonald shows how difficult it is to make us heed the imagination, whether we are empiricists like Curdie, greedy materialists like the people of Gwyntystorm, or narcissists like Agnes in *The Wise Woman*.

In *The Princess and the Goblin*, although the goblins are seen as evil and are destroyed, the symbolism of the book suggests that they are an essential part of Princess Irene's own mind, as of any human mind, and not to be denied. Yet here we see the "higher" imagination destroy the lower, as though the one could exist without the other. The "happy ending" in which the princess is saved from the goblins is false to the mental symbolism of the book—is, in short, *voulu*. By contrast, *The Wise Woman* refuses any such evasion. Of the two initially wicked children taken from their homes to reform them, there is some hard-won success with one girl and failure with the other. All the powers of the divine imagination represented in the wise woman and her strange cottage cannot overcome the rooted pride of Agnes. In the last book of the four, *The Princess and Curdie*, we go still further. Here we deal no longer with individuals, but with a whole corrupt society founded on greed and materialism. *The Wise Woman* ended with the prospect of further attempts being made on the obdurate Agnes, but there is no cure for collective materialism in this world, only putatively in the next. All that can be done here is to rid the world of this corruption by destroying it.

It would have been so easy for MacDonald to simplify, to offer only the happy view, to sink from the imagined to the imaginary. Diamond could have changed the world about him for better; the vision of a universe founded in God could have been left unchallenged. Perhaps though the self-satisfaction of Agnes in *The Wise Woman* is as yet too deep-rooted to be displaced; and it is hard to conceive any ready reformation of the selfish citizens and counsellors of Gwyntystorm in *The Princess and Curdie*.

But if the imagination cannot often transform the world for the better, every one of these fantasies insists that it is the truest thing that exists in life. In *The Princess and the Goblin*, Irene's grandmother, who changes during Irene's meetings with her from old woman to beautiful and queenly lady surrounded by the stars of infinite space, is far more real than anything the young princess has ever known. So too with grandmother in *The Princess and Curdie*; while the dog Lina and the other grotesque creatures witness to a realm of spiritual reality deeper than this one. The book may end in a desolate manner with Gwyntystorm destroyed and wild nature dominant, but we know also that beyond that lies a more lasting dimension of the spirit. *The Wise Woman* shows how our moral choices are ultimately metaphysical: if we make self the lodestar of our lives, we belong with nothingness, but if we subdue the self for another we may be welcomed into the community of heaven.

If the aim of the imagination is harmony,[9] then separation is its opposite. In *The Princess and the Goblin*, the different faculties of the mind are for long cut off from one another. In *At the Back of the North Wind*, there is a gulf between this world and the next, and between too-present reality and dream. Selflessness struggles with selfishness in *The Wise Woman*. Greed and materialism war with imagination and service in *The Princess and Curdie*, where we have a kingdom of self-serving egos opposed by a group of people who help others. The christening curses bestowed on two princesses, in "The Light Princess" and "Little Daylight," sever them from normal experience. The fairies steal a girl and then a boy in from their parents in "The Carasoyn," and also in "Cross Purposes"; and a giant steals greedy children in "The Giant's Heart."

More general separation, of the conscious self from the unconscious, is found in "Little Daylight": the royal court has cut itself off from the wild woods about it that symbolize the uncontrolled imagination. "Photogen and Nycteris," with Photogen confined to the light and Nycteris to the darkness, epitomizes this idea of the reduced or divided self. Each on his or her own is inadequate, and must come together to make a wedded whole of light and dark, conscious and unconscious. Indeed, a prime theme in the fairy tales is the inadequacy of the self on its own: princesses must marry princes. The solitude of the various wicked fairies and witches is part of what is bad about them. The selfish isolation of the citizens of Gwyntystorm is a threat to civil and supernatural society alike.

MacDonald said, "Two at least are needed for oneness."[10] In MacDonald's thinking, relationships are at the heart of God's universe, which is a network of singular beings created out of love. We exist because of God's

---

9. MacDonald, "The Imagination," *A Dish of Orts*, 35.
10. MacDonald, *Unspoken Sermons*, 298, 428.

Conclusion

delight in a multi-faceted creation: and as all its different parts are held together in love, so must we learn to come into this commonwealth of being. An element of "two-ness" is almost always found in MacDonald's children's fantasies. There are Diamond and North Wind, Irene and her grandmother, Irene and Curdie, even Rosamund and Agnes; and in the shorter tales, Buffy-Bob and Tricksy-Wee, Mossy and Tangle, Photogen and Nycteris, Alice and Richard. Compare these with the single central figures in Charles Kingsley, Lewis Carroll, or Mrs J. H. Ewing.

In "Cross Purposes," the theme is not just the distinguishing of reality from illusion but also the growing relationship between self-giving commoner Richard and snobbish squire's daughter Alice. The lifelong partnership of Mossy and Tangle is part of "The Golden Key," but more than that is Tangle's deepening relationship with the world around her. In "The Shadows," it is not so much Ralph Rinkelmann who relates to the shadows as they that relate to him, befriending him and showing him their lives. "Photogen and Nycteris" portrays the coming together of the Day Boy and the Night Girl, and of the sun and moon. The growing friendship of Irene with her grandmother and with Curdie is at the heart of *The Princess and the Goblin*, as is that of young Diamond and North Wind in *At the Back of the North Wind*.

As we read these children's fairy tales, several of them also begin to relate to one another. "Little Daylight" deals with a confinement to night that is paralleled in "Photogen and Nycteris." Curdie digging up into the wine cellar of the palace of Gwyntystorm in *The Princess and Curdie* recalls the goblins burrowing their way into the wine cellar of Irene's house in *The Princess and the Goblin*. Many influences spread out from "Cross Purposes," the first of the fairy tales written. Alice and Richard, silly girl and sensible boy in this story, are like Tangle and Mossy at the beginning of "The Golden Key," and both stories start on the borders of Fairyland, although "No mortal, or fairy either, can tell where Fairyland begins and where it ends."[11] Again at one point in "Cross Purposes," Richard and Alice go up stairs leading right into a perpendicular rock wall in front of them: this also recalls the similar mountain wall in "The Golden Key" into which Mossy goes after steps appear before him.[12] The little boy that Rosamond accidentally knocks into a lake and drowns in *The Wise Woman* recalls Alice lying beneath the water looking as though she is drowned in "Cross Purposes"; in

---

11. MacDonald, *The Complete Fairy Tales*, 104.
12. MacDonald, *The Complete Fairy Tales*, 115–16, 143.

both cases the one child stares upwards through the water while the other looks down from a boat. And, of course, there is the drowned prince looking upwards through the water at the Princess in "The Light Princess." The huge tree the children climb in "The Giant's Heart" is like the equally large one climbed in "Cross Purposes," and in both stories the children meet a pompous owl there. These similar features in several tales invite us to see how they are also changed in each new context; but more than this they show the tales spreading out tendrils of relationship among one another, to form a kind of family of faërian experiences that mirrors the nature of the divine universe.

Appendix A

On subgroups of the shorter fairy tales, see Gwen Watkins, "A Theologian's Dealings with the Fairies," 5–14; Jack Zipes, *Fairy Tales and the Art of Subversion,* 104–9; Michael Mendelson, "The Fairy Tales of George MacDonald and the Evolution of a Genre," 31–49; Dieter Petzold, "Maturation and Education in George MacDonald's Fairy Tales," 10–24; F. Hal Broome, "Dreams, Fairy Tales and the Curing of Adela Cathcart," 6–18; Nancy Mellon, "The Stages in Adela Cathcart's Cure," 26–43. Watkins looks at several of the fairy tales for their reflection of MacDonald's views and their recurrent symbols. Zipes considers three tales in terms of their subversions of the fairy tale and contemporary attitudes to sexual stereotypes and the education of children. Mendelson focuses on three tales to show how MacDonald modifies the traditional fairy tale genre in them. Broome and Mellon are concerned with the three stories published in *Adela Cathcart*—"The Light Princess," "The Shadows," and "The Giant's Heart." Petzold's topic of maturation also involves him with three tales.

Appendix B

In her "*Kore* Motifs in *The Princess and the Goblin*," in McGillis, ed., *For the Childlike*, 169–82, Nancy-Lou Patterson argues that MacDonald uses the myth of Demeter and Persephone and the Jungian interpretations of it as the basis of a maturation story in which the Princess Irene grows from child to adult, in the process defeating her lower subconscious (the goblins) and aligning herself with the higher values of her grandmother. In several striking ways the myth does indeed fit: Irene's mother dies during the story and Irene will be the new queen, there is much sense of gardens and flowers, there is a crude nurse, like Iambe in the myth, and there is an underworld to which the princess descends—but then it is the Ariadne myth that has to be added as source for the fact that it is not Irene who like Persephone has to be rescued, but she who does the rescuing, of the miner Curdie. And of course Persephone had to return to Hades for part of the year, where Irene is completely freed from the goblins. Maturation story there certainly is here, but to link it too closely to the myth so suggestively behind it is mistaken. During the story Irene's mother dies, and Irene takes on her role. In his "The Diamond in the Ashes: A Jungian Reading of the 'Princess' Books," in *For the Childlike*, 183–94, Joseph Sigman also reads the story in the light of the Persephone myth, and adds the story of Theseus and the labyrinth as the root of Curdie's experiences in the mines. However, he says both "Princess" books are focused on Curdie's maturation, and he downplays the role of Irene as a mediator to "Curdie's guide to the world within" (187). More generally, both these essays see the goblins as rightly destroyed, when in a sense they represent a part of humanity that has been degraded but which it cannot do without. Both also try to unify the "Princess" books into one story, making either Irene or Curdie the hero in both; where clearly Irene is the central figure in the first and Curdie in the second. And although both books are about the development of their central figures, *The Princess and the Goblin* also gives much pleasure in Irene as she *is*: a child of vivid character in many very human relationships.

Appendix C
Summary of Criticism of *The Wise Woman*

"Anon" discusses how far Rosamond has free choice in her moral improvement under the wise woman's instruction, and concludes that she shares in the construction of her new identity, not for the sake of self-determination, but so that she may re-educate her parents and prepare to serve her country as its future queen. Battin traces the duality of Princess Rosamond and shepherdess Agnes through their different moral narratives, concluding that Rosamond's moral change comes when she recognizes that the wise woman was once just such a lost princess as she, and that she herself can become a new wise woman. Holm's piece is the draft of a dissertation, in which she argues that the wise woman is a pattern of God in the Bible. She discusses how far the wise woman tries to break her subjects' wills and MacDonald's possible feminization of God. She also says that Agnes remains a nasty child, while Rosamond is on the road to becoming innocently child-like. More generally, she links various elements of the story to episodes in the Bible. Jarrar argues that the parents of the two girls are entirely responsible for their wicked natures, with a useful discussion of MacDonald's own parenting ethic, which was a mixture of Calvinist insistence on obedience and punishment, and loving treatment of the conforming child.[1]

---

1. See Greville MacDonald, *Reminiscences of a Specialist*, 27.

Works Cited

Abraham, Lyndy. *A Dictionary of Alchemical Imagery*. Cambridge: Cambridge University Press, 1998.

A.L.O.E. [A Lady of England]. *Fairy Know-a-Bit, or A Nut Shell of Knowledge*. London: Thomas Nelson, 1866.

Andersen, Hans Christian. *Wonderful Tales for Children*. Translated by Mary Howitt. London: Chapman and Hall, 1846.

Anderson, Celia Catlett. "*The Golden Key*: Milton and MacDonald." In *For the Childlike: George MacDonald's Fantasies for Children*, edited by Roderick McGillis, 87–97. Metuchen, NJ: Children's Literature Association, 1992.

Anon. "The Wise Woman as an Agent of Identity in George MacDonald's Story *The Wise Woman*." Web: library.taylor.edu; and eprints.worc.ac.uk/3196/1/WWasagentofidentityfinal1pdf.

Battin, Melba N. "Duality beyond Time: George MacDonald's 'The Wise Woman, or The Lost Princess: A Double Story.'" In *For the Childlike: George MacDonald's Fantasies for Children*, edited by Roderick McGillis, 207–18. Metuchen, NJ: Children's Literature Association, 1992.

Blake, William. *The Marriage of Heaven and Hell*. Etched and printed by Blake, 1789-90.

Brontë, Emily (as "Ellis Bell"). *Wuthering Heights, A Novel*. London: Thomas Newby, 1847.

Broome, F. Hal. "Dreams, Fairy Tales, and the Curing of Adela Cathcart." *North Wind* 13 (1994) 6–18.

Browne, Frances. *Granny's Wonderful Chair and Its Tales of Fairy Times*. London: Griffith and Farran, 1856.

Carlyle, Thomas. *Sartor Resartus: The Life and Opinions of Herr Teufelsdröckh*. Edited by Kerry McSweeney and Peter Sabor. Oxford: Oxford University Press, 1987.

Carpenter, Humphrey. *Secret Gardens: A Study of the Golden Age of Children's Literature*. London: Allen and Unwin, 1985.

Carroll, Lewis. *Alice in Wonderland*. London: Macmillan, 1865.

Chamisso, Adelbert von. *Peter Schlemihl's Miraculous Story* (*Peter Schlemihl's wundersame Geschichte*). Nuremberg: Johann Leonhard Schrag, 1814.

Chesterton, G. K. "Introduction." In Greville MacDonald, *George MacDonald and His Wife*, 9–15. London: Allen and Unwin, 1924.

Clifford, Lucy Lane. *Anyhow Stories, Moral and Otherwise*. London: Macmillan, 1882.

Coleridge, Samuel. *The Ancient Mariner*. First published in William Wordsworth and Samuel Taylor Coleridge, *Lyrical Ballads*, 2 vols. London: J. & A. Arch, 1798.

———. *Biographia Literaria or Biographical Sketches of My Literary Life and Opinions*. Edited by George Watson. London: Dent, 1956.
———. "Kubla Khan; or, A Vision in a Dream: A Fragment," 1797; first published in S. T. Coleridge, *Christabel: Kubla Khan, A Vision: The Pains of Sleep*. London: John Murray, 1816.
Cruikshank, George. *The Fairy Library*. London: Bell and Daldy, n.d.
Dallas, Eneas Streetland. *The Gay Science*. 2 vols. London: Chapman and Hall, 1866.
Darwin, Charles. *On the Origin of Species by Means of Natural Selection, or the Preservation of Favoured Races in the Struggle for Life*. London: John Murray, 1859.
Dasent, George Webbe. *Popular Tales from the Norse*. Edinburgh: Edmonston and Douglas, 1859.
Dickens, Charles. *A Christmas Carol*. London: Chapman and Hall, 1843.
———. "The Story of the Goblins Who Stole a Sexton." *The Pickwick Papers*. London: Chapman and Hall, 1836.
Ellenberger, Henri F. *The Discovery of the Unconscious: The History and Evolution of Dynamic Psychiatry*. London: Fontana, 1994.
Ewing, Mrs Juliana Horatia. *The Brownies and Other Tales*. London: SPCK, 1871.
Fouqué, Friedrich de la Motte. *Undine: Eine Erzählung*. Berlin: Hitzig, 1811.
Gatty, Margaret. *The Fairy Godmothers and Other Tales*. London: George Bell, 1851.
Grimm, J. and W. Grimm. *German Popular Stories Translated from the Kinder und Haus Märchen*. Collected by M. M. Grimm from Oral Tradition. 2 vols. Translated by Edgar Taylor. London: C. Baldwin, 1823, 1826.
Hastings, A. Waller. "Social Conscience and Class Relations in MacDonald's 'Cross Purposes.'" In *For the Childlike: George MacDonald's Fantasies for Children*, edited by Roderick McGillis, 75–86. Metuchen, NJ: Children's Literature Association, 1992.
Hoffmann, E. T. A. "The Golden Pot: A Modern Fairy Tale" ("Der Goldne Topf: Ein Märchen aus der neuen Zeit"). First published in Hoffmann, *Fantasy Pieces in the Manner of Callot (Fantasiestücke in Callot's Manier)*, 4 vols., vol. 3, 79–228. Bamberg: Kunz, 1814–15.
Hogg, James. *The Private Memoirs and Confessions of a Justified Sinner, Written by Himself*. London: Longman, Hurst, Rees, Orme, Brown and Green, 1824.
Holm, Deborah. "Tendering Greatness: George MacDonald's *The Lost Princess* and the Bible." *North Wind* 32 (2013) 85–118.
Houghton, Walter E. *The Victorian Frame of Mind, 1830–1870*. New Haven, CT: Yale University Press, 1957.
Jarrar, Osama. "Children's Fiction Discourse Analysis: The Critique of Victorian Economics in George MacDonald's *The Princess and Curdie*." *North Wind* 29 (2010) 52–65.
———. "Language, Ideology, and Fairy Tales; George MacDonald's Fairy Tales as a Social Critique of Victorian Norms of Sexuality and Sex Roles." *North Wind* 28 (2009) 33–49.
———. "*The Wise Woman, or The Lost Princess: A Double Story*: A Critique of Victorian Parenting." *North Wind* 32 (2013) 61–84.
Johnson, Kirstin Jeffrey. "The Progressive Key: A Study of Bunyan's Influence in MacDonald's 'The Golden Key.'" *North Wind* 16 (1997) 69–75.
Keary, Annie, and E. Keary. *Little Wanderlin and Other Fairy Tales*. London: Macmillan, 1865.

Works Cited

Kingsley, Charles. *The Water-Babies: A Fairy Tale for a Land-Baby.* 2nd ed. London: Macmillan, 1864.
Kingsley, Frances E., ed. *Charles Kingsley, His Letters and Memories of his Life.* 2 vols. London: Kegan Paul, 1876.
Lewis, C. S., ed. *George MacDonald: An Anthology.* London: Bles, 1946.
———. *The Magician's Nephew.* London: Bles, 1955.
———. *Perelandra.* London: John Lane, The Bodley Head, 1943.
———. *The Voyage of the "Dawn Treader."* London: Bles, 1953.
Lytton, Bulwer. *The Coming Race.* Edinburgh: Blackwood, 1871.
MacDonald, George. *Adela Cathcart.* London: Hurst and Blackett, 1864.
———. *Alec Forbes of Howglen.* London: Hurst and Blackett, 1865.
———. *At the Back of the North Wind.* Edited by Roderick McGillis and John Pennington. Peterborough, ON: Broadview, 2011.
———. *The Complete Fairy Tales.* Edited by U. C. Knoepflmacher. London: Penguin, 1999.
———. *Dealings with the Fairies.* London: Alexander Strahan, 1867.
———. *A Dish of Orts: Chiefly Papers on the Imagination, and on Shakespeare.* London: Sampson Low Marston, 1893.
———. "The Fantastic Imagination." Introduction to *The Light Princess and Other Fairy Tales*, 1893. Reprinted in *A Dish of Orts: Chiefly Papers on the Imagination, and on Shakespeare*, 313–22. London: Sampson Low Marston, 1893.
———. *George MacDonald in the Pulpit.* Whitethorn, CA: Johannesen, 1996.
———. *Guild Court.* London: Hurst and Blackett, 1868.
———. "The Haunted House." In *A Threefold Cord: Poems by Three Friends,* edited by George MacDonald. London: privately printed, 1883.
———. *The Hope of the Gospel* and *Miracles.* Whitethorn, CA: Johannesen, 1995.
———. "The Imagination," 1867. Reprinted in MacDonald, *A Dish of Orts: Chiefly Papers on the Imagination, and on Shakespeare*, 1–42. London: Sampson Low Marston, 1893.
———. "Preface." In *The Light Princess and Other Fairy Tales.* New York: Putnam, 1893.
———. *Lilith: A Romance.* London: Chatto and Windus, 1895.
———. *Phantastes, A Faerie Romance.* London: Smith, Elder, 1858.
———. *Phantastes and Lilith.* London: Gollancz, 1962.
———. *The Portent: A Story of the Inner Vision of the Highlanders, Commonly Called the Second Sight.* London: Smith, Elder, 1864.
———. *The Princess and the Goblin and Other Fairy Tales.* Edited by Shelley King and John B. Pierce. Peterborough, ON: Broadview, 2014.
———. *The Princess and the Goblin and The Princess and Curdie.* Edited by Roderick McGillis. Oxford: Oxford University Press, 1990.
———. *Ranald Bannerman's Boyhood.* London: Strahan, 1871.
———. *Robert Falconer.* London: Hurst and Blackett, 1868.
———. "Shelley," 1860. Reprinted in *A Dish of Orts: Chiefly Papers on the Imagination, and on Shakespeare*, 264–81. London: Sampson Low Marston, 1893.
———. *Sir Gibbie.* London: Hurst and Blackett, 1879.
———. "A Sketch of Individual Development," 1880. Reprinted in *A Dish of Orts: Chiefly Papers on the Imagination, and on Shakespeare*, 43–76. London: Sampson Low Marston,1893.
———. *Unspoken Sermons, Series I, II, III.* Whitethorn, CA: Johannesen, 1997.
———. *Wilfrid Cumbermede.* London: Hurst and Blackett, 1872.

Works Cited

MacDonald, Greville. *George MacDonald and His Wife.* London: Allen and Unwin, 1924.

———. *Reminiscences of a Specialist.* London: Allen and Unwin, 1932.

Manlove, Colin. "George MacDonald and the Fairy Tales of Francis Paget and Frances Browne." *North Wind* 18 (1999) 17–32.

———. "George MacDonald and Friedrich de la Motte Fouqué." *Wingfold* 104 (2018) 5–10.

———. "MacDonald and Kingsley: A Victorian Contrast." In *The Gold Thread: Essays on George MacDonald*, edited by William Raeper, 140–62. Edinburgh: Edinburgh University Press, 1990.

———. *Modern Fantasy: Five Studies.* Cambridge: Cambridge University Press, 1975.

———. *Scotland's Forgotten Treasure: The Visionary Romances of George MacDonald.* Aberdeen: Aberdeen University Press, 2016, and worksofmacdonald.com, 2018.

———. *Scottish Fantasy Literature: A Critical Survey.* Edinburgh: Canongate Academic, 1994.

Marshall, Cynthia. "Reading 'The Golden Key': Narrative Strategies of Parable." In *For the Childlike: George MacDonald's Fantasies for Children*, edited by Roderick McGillis, 99–109. Metuchen, NJ: Children's Literature Association, 1992.

McGillis, Roderick, ed. *For the Childlike: George MacDonald's Fantasies for Children.* Metuchen, NJ: Children's Literature Association, 1992.

———. "Language and Secret Knowledge in *At the Back of the North Wind.*" In *For the Childlike: George MacDonald's Fantasies for Children*, edited by Roderick McGillis, 145–59. Metuchen, NJ: Children's Literature Association, 1992.

———. "'Outworn Liberal Humanism': George MacDonald and 'The Right Relation to the Whole.'" In *Behind the Back of the North Wind: Critical Essays on George MacDonald's Classic Children's Book*, edited by John Pennington and Roderick McGillis, 82–89. Hamden, CT: Winged Lion, 2011.

Mellon, Nancy. "The Stages in Adela Cathcart's Cure." *North Wind* 15 (1996) 26–43.

Mendelson, Michael. "The Fairy Tales of George MacDonald and the Evolution of a Genre." In *For the Childlike: George MacDonald's Fantasies for Children*, edited by Roderick McGillis, 31–49. Metuchen, NJ: Children's Literature Association, 1992.

Milton, John. "Comus, A Mask Presented at Ludlow Castle, 1634." First published in *Poems of Mr John Milton both English and Latin, Compos'd at several times.* London: Humphrey Moseley, 1645–46.

———. "Il Penseroso" (1631). First published in *Poems of Mr John Milton both English and Latin, Compos'd at several times.* London: Humphrey Moseley, 1645–46.

Morris, William. "Lindenborg Pool." *Oxford and Cambridge Magazine*, September 1856.

Mulock, Dinah (afterwards Craik). *The Little Lame Prince and His Travelling Cloak—A Parable for Young and Old.* London: Daldy Isbister, 1875.

Novalis (Friedrich von Hardenberg). *Schriften.* Edited by Paul Kluckhohn and Richard Samuel. 3 vols. Stuttgart: Kohlhammer, 1960–68.

Paget, Francis E. *The Hope of the Katzekopfs; or, The Sorrows of Selfishness.* 2nd ed. London: Joseph Masters, 1847.

Paley, William. *Natural Theology: or Evidences of the Existence and Attributes of the Deity.* London: J. Faulder, 1802.

Patterson, Nancy-Lou. "Kore Motifs in *The Princess and the Goblin.*" In *For the Childlike: George MacDonald's Fantasies for Children*, edited by Roderick McGillis, 169–82. Metuchen, NJ: Children's Literature Association, 1992.

Works Cited

Pennington, John. "Alice at the Back of the North Wind, Or the Metafictions of Lewis Carroll and George MacDonald." In *Behind the Back of the North Wind: Critical Essays on George MacDonald's Classic Children's Book*, edited by John Pennington and Roderick McGillis, 52–62. Hamden, CT: Winged Lion, 2011.

Pennington, John, and Roderick McGillis, eds. *Behind the Back of the North Wind: Critical Essays on George MacDonald's Classic Children's Book*. Hamden, CT: Winged Lion, 2011.

Petzold, Dieter. "Maturation and Education in George MacDonald's Fairy Tales." *North Wind* 12 (1993) 10–24.

Poe, Edgar Allan. "Fall of the House of Usher." *Burton's Gentleman's Magazine*, 1839. Reprinted in E. A. Poe, *Tales of the Grotesque and Arabesque*, 75–103. Philadelphia: Lea and Blanchard, 1840.

Pope, Alexander. *The Rape of the Lock*. In *The Works of Mr Alexander Pope*. London: Bernard Lintot, 1717.

Prickett, Stephen. *Romanticism and Religion: The Tradition of Coleridge and Wordsworth in the Victorian Church*. Cambridge: Cambridge University Press, 1976.

Raeper, Willam. *George MacDonald*. Tring, UK: Lion, 1987.

———, ed. *The Gold Thread: Essays on George MacDonald*. Edinburgh: Edinburgh University Press, 1990.

Reis, Richard. *George MacDonald's Fiction: A Twentieth-Century View*. Eureka, CA: Sunrise, 1988.

Robb, David S. *George MacDonald*. Edinburgh: Scottish Academic Press, 1987.

Rossetti, Christina. *Speaking Likenesses*. London: Macmillan, 1874.

Rowling, J. K. *Harry Potter and the Deathly Hallows*. London: Bloomsbury, 2007.

Ruskin, John. *The King of the Golden River*. Written in 1841. London: Smith, Elder, 1851.

Schenkel, Elmar. "Antigravity: Matter and the Imagination in George MacDonald and Early Science Fiction." *North Wind* 14 (1995) 46–56.

Shaberman, Raphael B. *George MacDonald: A Bibliographical Study*. Detroit, MI: St Paul's Bibliographies and Omnigraphics, 1990.

Shakespeare, William. *Coriolanus*.

———. *Hamlet*.

———. *Henry V*.

———. *A Midsummer Night's Dream*.

———. *The Tempest*.

Sidney, Philip. "A Defence of Poesy," 1583. In *Literary Criticism: Plato to Dryden*, edited by Allen H. Gilbert, 404–61. Detroit, MI: Wayne State University Press, 1962.

Sigman, Joseph. "The Diamond in the Ashes: A Jungian Reading of the 'Princess' Books." In *For the Childlike: George MacDonald's Fantasies for Children*, edited by Roderick McGillis, 183–94. Metuchen, NJ: Children's Literature Association, 1992.

Sinclair, Catherine. "Uncle David's Nonsensical Story of Giants and Fairies." *Holiday House: A Book for the Young*, 197–214. London: Ward, Lock, 1839.

Smith, Lesley Willis. *The Downstretched Hand: Individual Development in George MacDonald's Fantasies for Children*. Hamden, CT: Winged Lion, 2018.

———. "Old Wine in New Bottles: Aspects of Prophecy in George MacDonald's *At the Back of the North Wind*." In *For the Childlike: George MacDonald's Fantasies for Children*, edited by Roderick McGillis, 161–68. Metuchen, NJ: Children's Literature Association, 1992.

———. "MacDonald's Crystal Palace: Diamond and Rubies, Coal and Salt in *At the Back of the North Wind*." *North Wind* 34 (2015) 13–57.

[Southey, Robert] "The Story of the Three Bears." In *The Doctor*, vol. 4, 318–26. London: Longman, Rees, 1837.

Southwell, Robert. "The Burning Babe," 1595. First privately printed after Southwell's execution in [Robert Southwell] *St. Peter's Complaint,* 1595.

Spenser, Edmund. *The Faerie Queene*. 2 vols. London: Ponsonby, 1590, 1596.

Stevenson, Robert Louis. *Strange Case of Dr Jekyll and Mr Hyde*. London: Longman, Green, 1886.

Sundmark, Bjorn. "Travelling Beastward: An Ecocritical Reading of George MacDonald's Fairy Tales." *North Wind* 27 (2008) 1–15.

Tanner, Tony. "Mountains and Depths—An Approach to Nineteenth-Century Dualism." *Review of English Literature* III (1962) 51–61.

Tennyson, Alfred Lord. "The Palace of Art." In *Poems*. 2 vols. London: Edward Moxon, 1832; revised in the expanded edition of *Poems* in 1842.

Thackeray, William Makepeace (as M. A. Titmarsh). *The Rose and the Ring, or The History of Prince Giglio and Prince Bulbo*. London: Newnes, 1855.

Watkins, Gwen. "A Theologian's Dealings with the Fairies." *North Wind* 7 (1988) 5–14.

Williams, Charles. "The Death of Good Fortune," 1939. Reprinted in Charles Williams, *Collected Plays*, edited by John Heath-Stubbs, 177–94. London: Oxford University Press, 1963.

Wolff, Robert Lee. *The Golden Key: A Study of the Fiction of George MacDonald*. New Haven, CT: Yale University Press, 1961.

Yonge, Charlotte, ed. "Introduction" to Friedrich de la Motte Fouqué, *Sintram and His Companions*. Cabin John, MD: Borgo, 2002.

Zaitchik, Mark. "Preface" to George MacDonald, *The Wise Woman, A Parable*. New York: Garland, 1977.

Zipes, Jack. *Fairy Tales and the Art of Subversion: The Classical Genre for Children and the Process of Civilisation*. New York: Routledge, 1991.